2.5
Minute
Ride

and

101
Humiliating
Stories

2.5 Minute Ride

and

101 Humiliating Stories

Lisa Kron

Theatre Communications Group
New York

2.5 Minute Ride and *101 Humiliating Stories* is published by Theatre Communications Group, Inc., 355 Lexington Ave., New York, NY 10017–6603.

This publication is made possible in part with public funds from the New York State Council on the Arts, a State Agency.

Theatre Communications Group wishes to acknowledge the Jerome Foundation for helping to make this publication possible.

TCG books are exclusively distributed to the book trade by Consortium Book Sales and Distribution, 1045 Westgate Dr., St. Paul, MN 55114.

Library of Congress Cataloging-in-Publication Data

Kron, Lisa
[2.5 minute ride]
2.5 minute ride ; and, 101 humiliating stories / by Lisa Kron.—1st ed.
p. cm.
ISBN 1-55936-181-6 (pbk. : alk. paper)
1. Jewish lesbians—Drama. 2. Jewish women—Drama. 3. Lesbians—Drama. 4. Monologues. I. Title: 2.5 minute ride ; and, 101 humiliating stories. II. Title: Two and a half minute ride. III. Title: Two point five minute ride. IV. Kron, Lisa. 101 humiliating stories. V. Title: 101 humiliating stories. VI. Title.

PS3561.R584 A615
812'.6—dc21   00-037755

Book design and typography by Lisa Govan
Cover photos by Kristina LeGros
Cover design by Susan Mitchell

First edition, June 2001

For my family who generously let me use their lives and haven't yet disowned me.

For The Five Lesbian Brothers who took me apart and put me back together as a better actor and something closer to a writer.

Most especially for Peg Healey—who has given me the gift of true devotion as well as all of the best ideas.

Contents

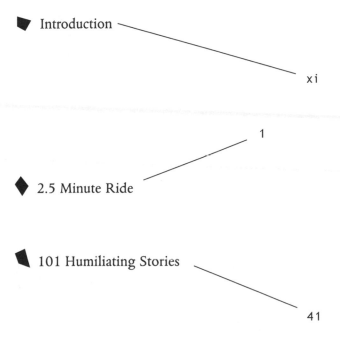

Introduction — xi

2.5 Minute Ride — 1

101 Humiliating Stories — 41

Acknowledgments

My thanks to the East Village performance spaces that existed in the mid-1980s where I wandered into a career as a solo performer—in particular, the W.O.W. Café, my home for many years; Dixon Place, where all my shows have been nurtured through their babyhoods; and Performance Space 122, which gave me my first longer runs and a professional step up.

Thanks to all at International Production Associates who kept faith in me and my work even when no one was booking it.

Thanks to New York Theatre Workshop—a true creative home; Michael Grief and the La Jolla Playhouse who took a chance on *2.5 Minute Ride* based on a twenty-minute reading; David Binder who, with great generosity, made it possible for me to rework the show in front of a New York audience; and The Joseph Papp Public Theater/New York Shakespeare Festival who gave the show the production I had dreamed of.

Most especially I thank Lowry Marshall who collaborated on the development of *2.5 Minute Ride* and Jamie Leo who collaborated on the development of *101 Humiliating Stories*. Both of them pushed me to do better work than I had done before, and each piece bears the imprint of their insight and considerable talents.

Introduction

My early solo shows were compilations of strung together anecdotes, low-rent versions of big musical numbers along with character bits and some short comic pieces made with film and slides. Two goals fueled this work, one was to really understand how to make an audience laugh. The other was to fully exploit and enjoy the development of my persona as a glamorous, all-singing, all-dancing lesbian ingenue—a possibility which was opened to me at the W.O.W. Café, that hotbed of sexy lesbian performance, and which had most definitely not existed in college or in the mainstream professional world where I was firmly put in my place by the label: "character actress."

After some years as the lesbian Lola Falana, as I called myself at that time, I was yearning to make work that would still be entertaining but would also have shape and resonance. I wanted to make solo work that would also be theater. It seemed to me that there were two rules I would have to follow to accomplish this. First, the goal of autobiographical material should not be to tell stories about yourself but, instead, to use the details of your own life to illuminate or explore something more universal. Second, the work should not merely be a series of recollections. There has to be a dynamic element—dramatic action and conflict. Something must *happen* in the course of the performance.

The greatest skill I have developed as a solo performer, and the one that has brought me the most joy, is my ability to speak directly to an audience—to draw on that energy an audience feels when they realize something is actually happening right now, tonight, in this very room. It is my goal to strive for total fluidity so that my performances expand and contract to incorporate any unexpected intrusions—like the ringing of a cell phone, or a particularly noticeable reaction. I don't want the audience to feel they are watching something that is going to play out the same way with or without them. Instead I want them to feel they are seeing something happen in this very moment—with them and because of them.

So it was natural, as I developed the two pieces that follow, that I would find the "action" of these plays in the very act of attempting to tell a story. And the "conflict" in each piece would be the derailing of the story's planned course, resulting in what appears to be a completely unanticipated revelation.

Each play employs a metaphorical devise which develops the conflict. In *101 Humiliating Stories* it is the overlay of the high school reunion (suggested to me by my partner Peg Healey, and developed by Jamie Leo). The phoned-in invitation to perform at this event sets in motion four speeches given to the class of 1979, which seem to bubble up from a subconscious well of anxiety tapped into by the very thought of revisiting high school. In *2.5 Minute Ride*, the slides (also suggested by Peg) serve as the catalyst. The journey taken in the piece reflects the six-year journey I took in creating it. I start out with the goal of telling the story of my father's life and experience, thus fulfilling my self-imposed duty as the witness and preserver of his lost world. In the telling, it begins to dawn on me that this is not a duty I can fulfill. The slides take on a life of their own and bring me to a broken-down place where I am entirely unmoored for a long, horrible moment until, out of this crisis, something new and unexpected surges out of me.

These two pieces differ in content, but they are alike in that they both seek out the awkward moment. They dwell in discomfort. It is here that humor can be found, of course, and it also allows for the exploration of great feeling while avoiding sentimentality. The work seeks the places where we stumble, where we are derailed by awkwardness, grandiosity, pretentiousness, vanity. It looks for the humanity lurking in the crevices of human behavior, and in so doing, creates a bond that makes room for certain assumptions to be challenged.

101 Humiliating Stories is not *about* me being a lesbian. But that was the assumption many of the audiences made upon first hearing me utter the "L" word. One of the delights of performing the show was feeling a house full of regional theatre subscribers travel from fear—that they were about to be harangued by a big, heavy-handed, man-hating message—to a surprised sense of identification and connection.

2.5 Minute Ride deals with the Holocaust—a subject an audience approaches with a tremendous amount of emotional assumption. It seems to me that in this age of Holocaust museums and memorials we have developed a way of responding to this most horrible of tragedies that, in fact, protects us from ever approaching its horror. We come to it with a prescribed attitude of reverence and awe. We know the outcome. We feel grief for the victims and heap shame on the perpetrators—and we feel secure in our ability to discern one from the other. As I considered my father's history, one of the things I became fascinated with was the difference between the stories describing the events of the Holocaust, and what it must have been like to actually experience those events.

Stories, of course, have a shape and a context. They are made up of elements handpicked from chaos to form sense. Life as we are living it has no shape. It's a matter of one foot in front of the other, with a very limited side-to-side view and no clear picture at all of what lies ahead. In any given moment we're likely to be driven by both our most generous selves and our most petty impulses. In *2.5 Minute Ride* I wanted to create a primary experience rather than a reflection of past experiences. Humor and horror are juxtaposed and you might not know for a second whether you are at Auschwitz or at the amusement park. The show does not tell you when to laugh and when to be solemn. The response is up to you.

Lisa Kron
Baltimore, Maryland
April 2001

2.5
Minute
Ride

Production History

The script for *2.5 Minute Ride* was developed through collaboration with Lowry Marshall.

2.5 Minute Ride premiered at La Jolla Playhouse on September 24, 1996. It was directed by Lowry Marshall. The set was designed by Richard Ortenblad, Jr., the lights by Trevor Norton and the sound and original music by Dan Froot. The production stage manager was Beth Robertson.

After changes to the script, a workshop production of *2.5 Minute Ride* opened in New York at Soho Rep in association with David Binder on April 2, 1997. Directorial consultants were Dan Hurlin and Peg Healey. The lighting design was by Susan A. White, sound design by Darron L. West and original music by Dan Froot. The production stage manager was Liza Dunn.

2.5 Minute Ride opened at The Joseph Papp Public Theater/New York Shakespeare Festival in New York on March 17, 1999. It was directed by Mark Brokaw. The set was designed by Allen Moyer, the lights by Kenneth Posner, the costume by Jess Goldstein, the sound by Darron L. West and original music by Dan Froot. The production stage manager was Bess Marie Glorioso.

Production Notes

2.5 Minute Ride is, on its face, a story about my family, in particular about my father, but it is my intention that the stories serve as a template, a framework into which audiences project their own relationships and experiences. The theatrical dynamic of the piece lies in the intersection between what is presented on stage and the imagination of the viewer. To that end, the design elements are intentionally devoid of specific or easily recognizable denotation, but the elements of light and sound do serve to keep the play moving, to push the performer from one story to the next.

There are four basic playing areas: upstage left there is a stool which serves as a place to set down the laser pointer and slide clicker. On it also rests the cigarette and a glass of water. The opening slides, and most of the subsequent slides as well, are described from this area. On the back wall is a black scrim upon which the slides are projected. There are no actual images but blank squares of colored light which are made with lighting specials rather than a projector. There is an area of light downstage left which is used for most of the stories about the wedding. Mid-stage right is an old-fashioned, school-library type, wooden straight-backed chair upon, and around which, stories about the trip to Germany and Auschwitz are generally told. The chair eventually comes to feel like a sort of surrogate for the car. Center stage is used for a variety of stories and descriptions. The matching of story location with stage location becomes less rigid as the piece progresses.

The music used for the production was original solo saxophone music composed by Dan Froot. It became clear fairly early in the development of the piece that, because the subject of the Holocaust is so overwhelmingly evocative, we wanted to steer clear of any music that would tap into the audience's well of previous emotional associations: Bach, for instance, or identifiably Jewish-sounding music such as klezmer. Dan's compositions worked extremely well because the nature of the piece moves abruptly between humor and horror and the saxophone is an instrument that naturally communicates at each end of that continuum.

Finally, a note about performance style. The piece juxtaposes stories of three different journeys. There are no written transitions between these stories. The intuitive performance choice is to create internal transitions with a pause, a breath, a drop of focus. But chief among the many great directorial contributions of Mark Brokaw was his insistence that I make the counterintuitive, but dynamic, choice to never pause or drop my focus. The thread of each story is kept suspended throughout the piece—not dropped and picked up again later. The sections do not end but are interrupted, overlapped by the next.

2.5 Minute Ride is written to be performed as if spoken for the first time directly to the people who are sitting in the audience. The energy which animates the performer is meant to be the same as that which animates a storyteller in real life—the desire to amuse, interest and move the listener. The sense should not be that the performer entered the room with every word planned out, but that the energy exchanged by the teller and the listener is building the story in the moment and taking it in unforeseen directions.

The audience hears the sound of a slide projector advancing to the next slide, as the lights come up on a woman holding a slide projector clicker and a laser pointer. She describes the following "slides," (not actually photographs, but squares of colored light) projected on a scrim. As she talks, she indicates what she sees with the pointer.

These are my grandparents. My father's parents. This, as you can see, is their wedding picture. I never knew them, actually. My father left his hometown in Germany in 1937, by himself, when he was fifteen years old, as a part of a program to get Jewish children out of Germany. I'm making a videotape about my father—about his experiences—well, actually about this trip we took together to his hometown in Germany and then to Auschwitz.

(Changes the slide with the clicker. The sound of an advancing slide projector is heard as a new square of light replaces the old one.)

Okay. This is my father's hometown. And here you can see we're looking down on the town from the clock tower. It was originally a walled city—I think you can see a little bit of the wall right here. *(Indicates with the laser pointer)* It's very beautiful, all these red roofs. My dad remembers every cobblestone in this city. He knows its history from its inception in the Middle Ages and I think he considers himself a part of that continuum. It was incredible, actually, when we were driving around. He can't see too well anymore but he'd say things to me like, "Now if you look to your left, you should see two dirt tracks," and there would be two dirt tracks, and he'd say, "That road was built by Napoleon." Then he'd say, "All right now we're going to go over a bump in the road," and we'd go over a bump, and then he'd say, "And if it's still there, you'll see to your right, a hill with a ditch at the bottom," and there would be a hill and a ditch, and he'd say, "I remember when I was a boy I used to ride my bike as fast as I could down that hill and try not to get caught by the group of boys who were chasing me but if I did I developed a method in which I would lie down in that ditch and pull one of the boys on top of me to use as a human shield."

(Changes the slide.)

Okay. This is my dad, you can see, and he's standing outside this apartment building where he lived when he was about three or four years old and here you can see that he's pointing up to this second-story window and he was telling me here about how, when he was about three or four years old, he put his head through the glass in that window. He said, "I planned it out very carefully. If I put my head through at the right angle and with the right amount of force it would pop right through the glass and then I could watch the parade going on down in the street." And I said, you know, "Did you hurt yourself?" And he said, "No, no. It worked out about the way I'd planned." We took this trip about seven or eight years ago, now. My dad had been back to Germany several times and I had been there once but we'd never gone together and this was something we always really wanted to do. So . . .

(Changes the slide.)

Okay, we're still in Germany. A little earlier in time, you can see here. This is my father and his father and they're here in the synagogue where his father was the cantor and also the teacher in the Jewish school. This was taken, I think, a few days before my dad left Germany to come to the United States. When he came here, he lived with a foster family in New Haven, Connecticut, and he received letters from his parents about once a week until one week, instead, he received a letter from the Red Cross informing him that his parents had been deported to the Litzmannstadt Ghetto which was in Poland. And that was the last time he heard directly from them.

(Changes the slide.)

Okay. This is something I might use in the video tape actually. This is a letter that my father received in 1947 from a man who had been with his parents in the Litzmannstadt Ghetto. I had it translated and it says, *(As she reads, she traces the lines with the pointer)* "Unfortunately, I must inform you that your parents were among the first transports sent to Auschwitz from the Ghetto." *(Traces ahead with the pointer)* And then skipping down here a little . . . "I was a close friend of your parents and I know quite well how attached to you they were and how often you were talked about." So, the other part of this trip was that we went to Auschwitz where neither one of us had ever been before. And the trip was extraordinary. It was so much more than either of us had imagined and when I returned I decided to make this video because my father has so many incredible stories and I wanted to make a record.

(Changes the slide.)

Okay. This is my Dutch "sister" Elizabeth—Elizabeth Klip— who was an exchange student who lived with our family when I was in college. She's extremely bright and so good hearted, you know, and a little high strung, I think you can see here, a little bit around the eyes. *(Indicates the eyes with the pointer)* She's completely devoted to my parents and she drove down from Holland to Germany to pick us up and take us to Auschwitz which is in Poland which was so great for us and a very nice vacation for her, too, as you can imagine.

(Changes the slide.)

Okay, this is my friend Mary who I asked to shoot this video for me. She's an accomplished videographer. She's done some wonderful pieces about her family and I asked her to accompany me and my girlfriend, my partner Peg, to Lansing, Michigan, where I grew up, where my parents still live, to shoot some interviews with my dad and then also to accompany us along with my entire extended midwestern family on our annual trip to the Cedar Point amusement park in Sandusky, Ohio, where my dad loves to ride the roller coasters, so we wanted to get that on tape as well, but anyway, here you can see Mary is in my mother's study, which is in the back hall of my parent's house, and here you can see she's showing me this little file cabinet of my mother's with all these little tiny drawers each meticulously labeled, and you can see here that she's pointing to this drawer marked, "stamps" and she was showing me here how my mother has organized all of her postage stamps with these little hand-made dividers by denomination. And she was saying to me here, "You know, your father's story is interesting but *this* would make a great video." My mother knows that everything has a purpose and throwing things away is a sin. She says, "You know, you all make fun of me for hanging on to everything, but when someone needs something they always come to me." My father always says, "I'd like to live in a stainless steel house with a drain in the middle."

(Changes the slide.)

Okay. Um. Okay, I don't know how this one got in here. This is Peg's family. This is from a huge family party I went to at Peg's parents' house several years ago. It was incredible. There were hundreds of them: Healeys, Dohertys, Flahertys . . . They were all healthy and Irish and good looking. They all played sports all day. And at one point in the afternoon, another one of the in-laws asked me, "Does your family have parties like this?" And I said, "No, no. My family's all either dead or crippled."

(Changes the slide.)

Okay. This is something that I might also use in the video. This is my dad here in his office, you can see—we were taping some interviews here—and behind him you can see this watercolor portrait that was done of him when he was an American GI. I think he paid a German soldier something like three packs of cigarettes to paint this for him. It's really so beautiful. My dad was drafted by the American army, after he managed to get himself declassified as an enemy alien, and then he was sent back to Germany where he worked as an army interrogator, questioning German . . . well, I was going to say POWs but they weren't really POWs. They were . . . arrestees, I guess you'd call them . . . or maybe detainees is a better word. If they were "arrestees" I guess they'd be Greek. *(Chuckles at her own stupid joke)*

(Changes the slide.)

Okay, this is my family—my mother's side of the family—the ones I actually know. And here you can see we're about to leave for Cedar Point—we're here in front of my cousins' house. There are about nine or ten of us who take this trip every year, and when we do we separate out into three great big American-made cars. You can see here my parents'

Mercury Marquis, and here's my cousins' Buick Skylark, and here I think you can see just the corner of my brother's full-sized Ford Econoline Van. Cedar Point is, I would say, about three, maybe three and a half, hours from Lansing, and when we take this trip every year we set aside three whole days so that we have a full day at the park and then an entire day for travel on either side. And during this epic cross-country trek these three vehicles remain in contact at all times with the use of—I think you can see a little bit here on my parents' dashboard—walkie-talkies. I brought this picture because my mother says that I exaggerate when I talk about the family but, I mean, look at the pictures.

My mother is horrified at the prospect of people in her house with video cameras and she keeps bringing up that 1970s PBS series on the Loud family. And on our second day in Michigan she takes all of us over to the Pilgrim House so that we can buy all new chairs for the living room. Now, my parents have been in a solidly upper-middle-class tax bracket for at least thirty-five years but they've never owned a piece of furniture that wasn't previously owned by someone else, but I think that it's the threat of immortality by video that brings out in my mother an almost irresistible urge to redecorate. And we buy all this brand new furniture. And that night, after everyone else has gone to sleep, my mother and I stay up and push big, big pieces of furniture back and forth and back and forth around the living room floor. My mom has these incredible, inexplicable swings in physical ability. One second she can barely hobble from her La-Z-Boy to the bathroom and the next second she's like Jack LaLanne pulling a sofa across the living room with a strap in her teeth.

I'm trying to remember how many times we actually went to Cedar Point as a family when I was growing up. It's occurring to me that it's one of those fake "traditions" my mother uses to get me to come home more often. Like how she asks me every year, "Are you going to make it home for

Christmas this year?" And I say, "I don't come home for Christmas. Mom. I have never come home for Christmas. We are not Christians. Stop trying to trick me!"

(Sound of a car passing. She leaves the clicker and pointer on the stool and crosses to chair. Sits.)

Elizabeth drives like a demon over pitch-dark Polish roads. Dad sits in the back and tells us stories. I ask questions. I keep my voice firm. I keep my crying to myself.

"Were you looking for your parents?"

"No, I had done that the summer before."

"And was it hard to accept it? Was it shocking?"

"No, I don't think it was hard to accept because I don't think I did accept it. I knew but I think somewhere I thought maybe they were still alive. I don't think I accepted it until a few years ago, in Lansing. It was the winter and it was so cold and I was shivering. In my coat. And I realized this would only happen to them once. They were old and they stood outside, lined up in the cold and they were of no use to anyone and they were killed."

(Crosses to center.)

At the entrance to the Magnum there are signs all over which say under no circumstances is this ride suitable for people who are elderly, diabetic or have heart conditions. I look at my father. He can't read the signs because, in addition to having all the conditions listed, he is also legally blind. I tell him what it says and I say, "Are you sure this is a good idea?" And he says, "I don't have to do anything. All I have to do is sit there." And then he pops a nitroglycerin in his mouth. "Well, then, why are you doing that?" I say. "Just in case." I try to get him to pretend to take another one so that Mary can tape him doing it. This might make a very nice video moment. But he says no because he's worried that if the girls who run the rides see him taking a pill they won't let him on.

(The sound of a car passing pulls her back to the chair. She sits.)

A horrible moment in the parking lot. We think they're going to make us pay to go in. No way, no way, no way. In the car we don't say anything to each other but it's clear to all of us that we can't pay an admission fee for Auschwitz. Oh. They're only charging us for parking. Well. Okay.

(Slightly dark, but energetic, sax music plays. She crosses to the "wedding area.")

My brother is getting married. In Peg's family when someone's getting married, her parents say, "Oh, isn't it exciting? They're so in love." In my family, when someone's getting married my parents say, "Well, I hope they know what they're doing. They seem to be crazy about each other." My brother lived on the third floor of my parents' house until a few years ago when my mother asked him to go live in the attic of my dead grandmother's house. Peg and I had spent a month living in that house the summer after my grandmother died, about seven or eight years ago, to help my mom organize an estate sale. The house was packed, floor to ceiling with things. Like, there was a whole room full of Avon my grandmother had bought because she felt sorry for the Avon lady. We tried to sell as much of her stuff as we could but there was just too much, and there was the added problem of my mother's attitude. When someone would ask for a lower price on something, my mother would snatch the item out of their hands and say, "I know exactly how much my mother paid for this item twenty-five years ago and if you don't want it for that price I'll just keep it myself." So now, eight years later, the house is still full of this stuff although it has all been organized on the first floor on steel shelving, along with the large collection of gay male pornography left by my grand-mother's brother, my great-uncle Robert, who also lived in the house, who was a horribly twisted and bitter old closet case who never had a cheerful or generous word to say to anyone. His two most often used phrases, actually, were, "My God in heaven" and "99.9% of the people," which he would combine into sentences sometimes, such as, "My God in heaven! 99.9% of the people who go to that breakfast bar over at the Big Boy restaurant just shovel the food into their mouths! *They just shovel it in!*" The month we stayed in Lansing to help out we lived in the house with him. He refused to learn Peggy's name and referred to her only as, "That girl you people call Peggy!" Anyway, now my uncle is dead and my brother lives in the house so that my mother can keep it insured. Peg says that David better never get in trouble with the law because he lives like a serial killer. "I mean look at the facts," she says, "he lives in the attic of his dead grandmother's house filled with gay male pornography because his mother makes him."

My brother met his fiancée on the computer. He wanted to meet a Jewish girl and he lives in Lansing, Michigan, so he signed onto America Online and went right to the Jewish sin-gles room where he got down to the business of finding a wife. Every girl seemed really great to him. I tried to figure out his standards. They seemed to me to be something like, "Well, she doesn't seem to have a criminal record. I think I'll marry her." Finally, though, finally, he met the right girl. Shoshi Rivkin from Brooklyn. They asked us to be brides-maids. "Yes, we'd love to!" we said, when they called to tell us they were engaged. It seemed like such a funny joke. A few days later we realized we had agreed to be *bridesmaids*. I, in particular, realized I had agreed to wear a matching outfit with my girlfriend. This seemed to me to be a special kind of nightmare. I called to tell Shoshi how terribly honored we were but we just couldn't be bridesmaids but we would be happy to sing. I don't know why I told her that. I wanted to write a funny song for the reception. Peggy was horrified. "What kind of a funny song?" she said: "David, we thought you were a neuter/until you met a girl on the computer?" Then they wanted us to sing a Hebrew song in the ceremony. Then they told us we couldn't sing because their rabbi is Orthodox and he told them that Orthodox men cannot be in the presence of a singing woman. They said they hoped we weren't offended by that. "Hey," I said, "it's your wedding and we want what you want." I'm trying to take my mother's advice. She says, "I'm just going to go to that wedding and pretend I'm watching a National Geographic special on TV." But I have a horrible vision. I can see myself at their wedding wearing a man's suit and chomping a big cigar and I'm afraid that every time the rabbi walks by I will compulsively sing at him, "There's No Business Like Show Business!"

(A new slide clicks into place. This brings her back to the stool. She picks up the laser pointer and describes the new "image.")

Ah. This is poor Mary standing on the exit stairs of the Iron Dragon. Under no circumstances would they let us bring a video camera on a roller coaster but one of the girls told us that Mary could go up the exit stairs and shoot from the platform on the other side. But when she got there they gave her a really hard time and she was getting really pissed off, you know, because these little high school amusement park girls were getting all snippy with her and making her stand in the sun and she already had that kind of aggravated look that lesbians get in amusement parks in Ohio. So she told me that I would have to go first and convince the girls to let her onto the exit platform. And I found a method that worked pretty well, actually. I'd say, "Can my friend shoot here?" And the girls would say, "Well . . . uh-uh." Then I'd say, "We're doing a documentary video about my father. He's a seventy-five-year-old, blind, diabetic Holocaust survivor with a heart condition." And they'd say, *(Full of wide-eyed, schoolgirl sympathy)* "Ooh. Oh. Okay." It's painfully easy to place the weight of the world right on a teenage girl's shoulders.

(Sound of a plane passing overhead. She crosses to stand next to the chair.)

We flew from Michigan to France, to save money, and then traveled by train to Germany. The train trip was a nightmare. Dad had brought four bags as if he was traveling with a valet when in fact there was only me. Also I couldn't read any of the signs because I don't speak German, and he speaks German of course, but he can't see to read them and so I had to sound them out. This was an exercise in pure humiliation. I'd say, *(Making a great effort to be clear but quiet enough to avoid attention. She has no idea how to pronounce these words)* "Waehlen . . . Sie . . . jetzt . . . die Vorwahl . . . und *(Long pause culminating in a deep sigh of impending defeat)* gewuenschte . . . Ruf . . . Rufnummer . . . " And he'd say, "What? Speak up. I can't hear you." And I'd think to myself, HOW'D YOU LIKE TO BE PUSHED OUT OF THE TRAIN, OLD MAN!?

(Crosses to center.)

There's nothing like watching someone else watch your family to really give you some perspective. I keep catching Peggy and Mary staring at various members of my family like this— *(Hands rush to her face and she staggers backward as if witnessing a scene of horror)* They don't understand why my family likes to come here. Now that they bring it up, I guess I don't really either. Three members of my family are—to use an expression I think you are not supposed to use anymore but it is the expression my family uses to describe itself—

"crippled." As in the phrase: "So crippled-up we can hardly walk." In addition to being crippled they are also in great, great pain. They gasp and moan with pain all day. It is in this state that my family, once a year, tackles a fifteen-acre amusement park. This year, along with her wheelchair, my Aunt Francie is also dependent on an oxygen tank which must be wheeled alongside of her. It's so hot that the park is nearly deserted and my mother and my aunt consider anything above fifty degrees a heat wave. The sad truth is that my family comes to Cedar Point for the food. I can't bear it. A few years ago, after a little therapy, I began to be aware that the women in my family often say things like: "Oh, I'm really not hungry. I couldn't eat a thing. I think I'll just have some pudding." Or: "I just need a little something light, maybe some pie." And as soon as we arrive at Cedar Point, Aunt Francie, true to form, says, "I really don't feel good. I think I need a hamburger." The day has just begun and already I'm feeling trapped, trapped, trapped with my family. I involuntarily leave my body and squish my whole self into my brain where a voice in my head is ranting: "A hamburger will not make you feel better! Shut up! Shut up about hamburgers! It's ten o'clock in the morning for God sakes! Eating the hamburgers at Cedar Point is probably what put you in that wheelchair in the first place!" My therapy brain kicks in. I think, Now, Lisa, this reaction seems a little extreme. Is it your aunt you are despising or the part of you that is capable of eating a hamburger at ten o'clock in the morning? These thoughts must be leaking out of my brain onto my face because I see Peggy giving me the "chill-out-it's-only-ten-o'clock" look! I try to reenter my body but when I do I see that Aunt Francie is eating—from out of her purse—several cold sausages left over from breakfast at the Bob Evans. I concentrate on making my face blank and just following Peggy, and I try not to think about how last night at the Friendly's my aunt went on for ten minutes to the waiter about what foods make her choke.

(Crosses back to the chair and sits.)

When Elizabeth doesn't eat she gets insane. *(We hear the sound of screeching car tires)* She drives up on curbs and the wrong way down one-way streets. I try to coax her to eat. "Would you like a cookie?" "No!" she says. "I can't stand those cookies. I can't even look at them anymore. They make me sick." And she hurls them into the back seat where my father looks bewildered, thinking something is blowing in through the windows. I say, "I think you're really hungry." This is so stupid. It's like when you're little and your mother says, "You're acting tired," which, I don't know about you, but inevitably made me furious. And Elizabeth yells at me, "I'M NOT HUNGRY! I'M JUST DRIVING BUT THIS COUNTRY IS STUPID AND POLISH PEOPLE ARE STUPID AND THERE'S NO FOOD HERE AND THAT'S FINE. I DON'T CARE. I'M NOT HUNGRY." As she continues this rant she picks up speed, at one point hitting about 65 miles per hour on a dirt road. She's right though. There is no food in Poland. Well, maybe there is, but they keep it a secret. Where are the big neon signs? That's my question. How do you locate food without big neon signs? I'm also sick of the little Dutch anise cookies we've been eating for three days although, unlike Elizabeth, that hasn't stopped me from eating them. "Wait, stop," I say, "there's a restaurant!" "No," Elizabeth says, "I don't care." "Elizabeth, honey, we have to eat something. Come on, Elizabeth, we have to go to the restaurant. Oh my God. Come on Elizabeth you have to stop the car. Elizabeth, stop this car! Elizabeth, stop this car NOW!" *(She reaches over with her foot and stomps on an imaginary break, as we hear the sound of a car screeching to a halt.)* Thank you.

We've found a Polish pizza parlor. There's only one thing on the menu. Pizza. We each order two pieces of this pizza even though we are fully aware of its nature: a piece of white toast with melted American cheese and ketchup poured on top. We eat the pizza and we like it. This might actually go over big in the Midwest where cheese is a vital component of every dish. No food is considered edible in the Midwest unless it's fried and covered with melted cheese. Health food in the Midwest is anything in a pita. Like a Big Mac in a pita would be considered health food in the Midwest. And so I settle back into my midwestern heritage and I enjoy the greasy, cheesy toast. I order a third.

(The sound of a new slide clicking into place brings her back up to the stool to describe the new "image.")

Okay, we're going back a little bit in time here. This is a picture from 1983, and here you can see me and my dad and we're standing in front of the Demon Drop which is a three-story free fall. Cedar Point is known as America's Roller Coast because it has more roller coasters than any other amusement park in America—and every year they add a new one. And in 1983 they added the Demon Drop and Dad asked me if I wanted to ride it. And I laughed. I thought he was joking because at that time my family didn't ride the roller coasters. We mostly stuck to the more handicapped accessible rides. Like the Riverboat Ride was one of our favorites, which is a scenic tour down the mighty quarter-mile long Cedar River where you pass a number of mannequins—you know, animated mannequins—engaged in a variety of activities like, oh, you know, playing the banjo, getting caught in the outhouse, engaging in a feud, a scalping, that sort of thing . . . But this first year of the Demon Drop, Dad asked and asked and asked about it. He brought it up in the morning at Jungle Larry's Safari and then again during lunch at Frontier Village and at the end of the day, when we were heading back to the parking lot via the Swiss Chalet Sky Ride, he asked about it again and all of a sudden it dawned on me: "Do you want to ride the Demon Drop?"

I said. And he said, "Oh. Well, if that's what would make you happy."

It's hard . . . it's hard to describe a three-story free fall. It's not bad, really. It's not good. It's just like— *(A sudden, shocked exhalation of all the air in her lungs, as if kicked in the stomach)* —When it was over, about a second and a half after it began, I was speechless, I was aghast. I looked at my dad. He was grinning. A crazy sort of a grin.

That first ride on the Demon Drop was the summer before he lost most of his vision. Before that time he had just a small blind spot in his left eye. Someone told me that my mother thought that maybe it was that first ride on the Demon Drop that caused the hemorrhage that took the rest of his center vision leaving him with just peripheral sight. All of a sudden the middle was gone. Only the edges remained. Dad doesn't think the Demon Drop caused his vision loss. And even if it did, he says, "The damage is done."

At his office we tape him showing us all the tools he has to help him see. The closed-circuit TV, the overhead projector and, of course, the big bag of eyeglasses worth $2,000, that he carries with him everywhere. He has one pair of thick half-glasses he uses so that he can sign a check or a credit card slip, and one pair of binoculars mounted on glasses frames that enable him to make out a telephone number written in big digits on a note pad and, of course, his ten-power monocular that lets him read a sign far away, word for word. He says to us, "It's interesting how the brain compensates. For instance, Lisa, where your head is, I see a . . . a flower pattern.

(Sound of church bells draws her attention. She crosses and stands behind the chair.)

In Poland we see men carting hay in horse-drawn wagons, old women digging potatoes, empty streets in run down cities. I thought I'd be so fascinated to see this world where the clock had stopped fifty years before but now, to my horror, I find I'm just like Edna from the World Apart Travel Agency in Lansing, Michigan who had said to me before I left, "Eastern Europe? Oh, cripes, that's depressing."

Where is the mall? That's what I'd love to see, the Polish mall where I could look at the different items in the Polish card shops and buy funny things to bring home for the cousins and for Peg. I'd feel so much better if I could just buy something. How did I end up in Poland anyway when where I really wanted to be was Polish Land where I could go to the Pierogi Hut and buy a kielbasa hero from a fresh-faced high school student. I don't speak Polish. I don't speak German either but at least when I was there I could tell where the words begin and end. Here I feel like I'm listening to gibberish. One time we stop at a bus stop to ask a man for directions and when he answers me I start to laugh. I laugh right in his face. I'm not laughing at him. I'm laughing at how absurd it is that I'm listening to him as if I had the vaguest idea what he is saying. He gestures that he wants to get into our car. He's going to ride with us so he can point us in the right direction. He directs us to his house. Then he gets out and says something like, "Blah, blah, blah. Pointy, pointy, point. Polish, Polish, Polish, Polish . . ."

It's a good thing Elizabeth has a sixth sense about where we're going. I'm supposedly the navigator, but in Poland I'm hopeless. The roads are all tiny and curvy and it's hard to identify which is which since they all seem to be spelled: C-Z-Y-C-N-Z-S-Y. But Elizabeth just glances at the map and she's off. Speeding us in the direction of Auschwitz.

(Sax music moves her to center and fades out as she begins to speak.)

What is my mother going to do about this wedding? This is exactly the kind of event she's been studiously avoiding for the past thirty years. In a certain way we wonder why my brother would even have a wedding when it means putting my mother in this situation? She hates ceremony. She hates ritual. She has a law that she never goes anywhere where you have to wear panty hose. And then there is the No Picture Rule. This is really the thing. This is the heart of the matter. We do not take pictures of my mother. And this isn't a joke. No sneaking up is allowed. We never, never take pictures of my mother and it's funny really, because she loves pictures of other people. She loves them so much that sometimes I think she would like to have a copy of every picture taken of every person she ever met. She can't bear to think of a moment being lost when it could have been recorded. *(To someone in the audience)* If you were ever recorded on video and you tell my mother about it she'll say, "Oh, I'd like to have a copy of that." So it's funny really, that she won't let us take pictures of her.

(A series of slides appears on the scrim. One dissolves into the next as she describes them.)

My mother looks girlish and womanish and very happy and she's beaming out of a tiny color photo in a big, blue picture hat. Behind her, my father, with his hand on her shoulder, purses his lips and rolls his eyes up, mugging away, unbeknownst to her. It is their wedding picture. There are a few pictures after that. Their trip to Europe. I was conceived in Venice, you know. (Well, not actually in Venice, but in the nearby town of Mestra where the hotels are a lot cheaper.) In these pictures she's windblown and beautiful and so happy. My dad is dark and mysterious. Thick dark hair. Huge brown eyes. Mom showed me letters he wrote to her when they were first married. Scores of them. Describing their life together. All written as if to someone else. "My new wife Ann and I are very much in love, etc . . ." He mailed them to her from the corner. Then there are some pictures of her as a young mother and then there are no more. She was still happy with her husband and she was happy with her two children but she was no longer happy with the way she looked and so that was the end of the pictures. And so there have been no pictures of my mother for a span of about thirty years.

(The last slide of the series disappears.)

I can't picture how she's going to cope with this wedding and I'm worried she's going to get sick, you know, really, really sick, and have to miss it. She told me she threw up during a midnight grocery shopping run at Meijer's Thrifty Acres. She seems okay about it . . . I don't know. She always told us when we were growing up that she wanted us to elope and I never had any doubt that she meant it. When I came out as a lesbian I'm sure one of her first thoughts was, Oh, thank God I won't have to go to her wedding.

(Sax music, beginning with a long plaintive note, interrupts her. She walks to the chair and sits.)

What month was it? October. It's so cold. Elizabeth's car has separate controls for heating the driver and the passenger. On my side, I've pushed the little lever all the way over to hot. I don't think we listened to much music. Oh no. We did. Bach. Seems appropriate for the night before Auschwitz. Dinner at the Orbis Hotel. Dad says, "How funny, tonight we're having a beer with dinner and tomorrow we'll be at Auschwitz." *(Music fades out)* Dad and I, we've been waiting for this our whole lives. We don't know how to feel. Tomorrow we'll be at the place where his parents' bodies lie. No, they were burned. Will we step on their ashes? Will we see a wooden palate where they slept? Will we kick a stone they also kicked? Will they be hovering above the place, watching us?

Are they waiting for their boy? Have they waited all this time for their little boy to come and say good-bye to them?

(Stands.)

I almost had a nervous breakdown before this trip. I lost a friend over it. She told me she was sick of hearing about it. She's an asshole, but I did sound like a broken record, I'm sure. But what will I do, I thought, if my father cries? I've never seen him cry. What if he falls to the ground and sobs and curses the heavens? On the one hand I think I have these maternal feelings toward him and on the other hand I couldn't handle it if I really have to hold him like I were his mother.

Oh. The room is full of hair. Is that my grandmother's hair? Is she here? Elizabeth is just pregnant and she feels sick. If you believe a baby can be marked, you shouldn't come to Auschwitz. A room full of eyeglasses. They stumbled off blind to their deaths. A room full of suitcases. The smell, ugh, the smell. A room full of artificial limbs.

The Israelis are here. A big group with a huge Israeli flag. Huge enough for my father to easily see all day the big blue Mogen David. What a blessing they're here today. He doesn't say too much but I know that these Israelis are his little safety valve. A reminder that the world of Auschwitz is no more. I'm glad they're here too, although after my initial feelings of comradeship, I'm just irritated all day with these irritating Israelis. If I get shoved one more time . . .

We read every word of every exhibit. I have to read them out loud to Dad, of course. "Okay. This is a poem by a woman named Zofia . . . *(Stumbles over the pronunciation)* Groch-o-wal-ska Abromowicz. *(Realizing he can't hear)* I'm sorry. *(She repeats herself significantly louder)* Abromowicz. It says: *(Continuing loudly)*

1944.

Wheels speed along the tracks
rushing toward the victory of crime,
transporting, transporting people to gas,
people to a cremator,
people to a petrol sprayed pyre.
Smoke floats, thick, foul smoke . . .

(Seeing the next line of the poem, her face crumples. Instead of the words, a sob comes out. She turns and covers her face.)

I bury my head in my father's shoulder to hide my contorted face. He pats my back. He's okay. He's a good dad. I feel all shaky and helpless. I pull myself together. Really! The day is just beginning. *(Turns back to face the poem)* I repeat the words that have undone me: "People burn people here."

(Pivots around to stand behind the chair.)

We go on the Mean Streak which is a new wooden roller coaster with a 2.5 minute ride. As soon as we take off, I know that it's a mistake. Dad is clinging to the bar and he has a look on his face like a horse in a fire. I feel like my teeth are rattling out of my head. I hold onto my dad's arm, trying to pump some kind of rays into his body that will keep him from having a heart attack. I think, Oh, my dear God, what have I done? This is really going to kill him. 2.5 minutes is a really long time on a roller coaster if you are having a good time. If you think the experience is killing your father it's a really, <u>really</u> long time. For a split second I can see Mary selling this videotape to *A Current Affair*. The lead-in will read: BIZARRE MURDER!!! LESBIAN FORCES BLIND HOLOCAUST VICTIM ON ROLLER COASTER! KILLS OWN FATHER! I'm so relieved when we get to the end I'm almost weeping. I want to carry him to the first-aid station. I wonder if he can walk. He stumbles out of the car. *(She stumbles to center)* Walks right up to the video camera, as if for a post-game interview, and says, "That one was the best." And asks me if I want to go again.

The first Auschwitz camp is like a college campus. Red brick buildings and swaying birch trees. A beautiful wrought iron fence with a sign that says: "arbiet macht frei" . . . *work will make you free.* You have to use your imagination here to comprehend what went on. In the afternoon we drive the three miles to the second camp—Birkenau. Here, you need no imagination. This one looks like what it was. It was sunny three miles away. Here there is no sun. This is malevolent ground. On the way in, I ask Dad and Elizabeth if they want a snack from the car. "No," they say. They can't eat here. I can. I feel defiant as I shove a cracker into my mouth and walk through the gates.

They give us a map and we go exploring. The day alternates between a feeling of horror and a feeling we're at Disney. We look at the map and say, "Well, where should we go next? To the pits where they buried bodies in mass graves or the fields where they piled them up and burned them." We have to laugh. We especially laugh at the bookstores which we refer to as the Auschwitz gift shop. They sell postcards there. "Greetings from Auschwitz, wish you were here." We make gruesome jokes about what gifts they might sell . . . lamp shades and soap. I actually go into one of the shops to buy a book but it's full of pictures of the pope and I turn around and walk out.

(There is a long, very long, still pause—an almost unbearable silence—as she realizes the thing she's about to say.)

I'd been so afraid I wouldn't feel anything here.

(The silence hangs as she realizes:)

I think that was my biggest fear.

(Then she gets drawn into the explanation of her memory.)

But when I enter the crematorium for the first time in my life I feel horror. Physical repulsion. I can feel my face contort, my lips pull back. In the gas chambers my father stops to take his two o'clock pill. This breaks my heart. I stand to the side and cry. Hard. I can feel . . . I can feel the bottom. It's clear to me now that everything in my life before this has been a shadow. This is the only reality: what happened to my father and his parents fifty years ago. Elizabeth sees me crying and says, "Oh, no."

(The following feels like an actual break from the play. The audience should have the disconcerting feeling that the woman has abandoned her performance persona and is speaking spontaneously and directly to them. As a result, the words change slightly with each audience. If someone answers one of the questions posed, that answer is acknowledged and incorporated.)

I don't know why I'm telling you this. You all already know what this looks like, right? You've seen these images before. You don't need me to describe this to you. You know, it's occurring to me that there's a fairly good chance there's someone sitting here who's been to Auschwitz before. And you don't need me to tell you what this looks like, do you? It's insulting, really. It's upsetting and it's insulting. Even if you've never been there you've seen these images before, right? In the movies—*Sophie's Choice* . . . *Schindler's List!* *Schindler's List!* Is there anyone sitting here right now who *didn't* see *Schindler's List? (Scans the audience for takers)* Really. Really. And you know what? That's exactly what it looks like when you go there. That movie was really well done. That's exactly what it looks like. If you missed the movies you've seen it on TV, right? On public television or the History Channel? Sometimes I feel like they show these images every fifteen minutes or something. You know the ones I'm talking about, the films from the liberation of the camps with the bulldozers and the bodies. Right? You all know what this looks like. I don't know what I'm doing. I feel like a cliché. I'm reminding myself, actually, of this crazy woman that I met this one time. She and I were seated together at this dinner and everyone else knew she was crazy but I had just arrived at this place and I did not know this and so, of course, I got into a conversation with her and she said to me, "Well, yes, my mother hated me. And she treated me like shit and she hit me and she's never had the slightest interest in any of my work but *that's not my point.*" That's how I feel right now. I feel like I'm evading the issue here but I don't know what the issue is. Yes! Yes! I wanted to tell you about our trip. No. No! *"That's not my point!"* I wanted to tell you about my father!

(Pause, stunned at her own revelation. All of a sudden the woman realizes she has totally exposed herself. Not sure how she got here or how to get out of it, she is at a total loss. She really has no idea what to say next. This should be a truly horrible moment.)

But what? Umm . . . I don't know. I really don't know. Uh . . . He's . . . a . . . guy. You know, he's an ordinary guy. He's a dad. He's my dad. *(Suddenly she comes downstage, almost into the audience, stepping disconcertingly into their space in her need to make this connection—to make them hear and understand what she is about to say)* Do you know what he told us when we were growing up? When we were growing up he told us many, many times, "If it weren't for the good fortune of being born a Jew I might have become a Nazi." And then he'd tell us this story: he'd gone to school with a boy named Lohmann who was the only other boy in his class at school who didn't wear a Hitler Youth uniform. My father wasn't allowed to wear one, of course, because he was a Jew, and he was beaten by the other boys regularly for that, but Lohmann didn't wear one because he refused. "I often wonder," my father would tell us when we were growing up, "I often wonder. If I had had the opportunity to wear that uniform if I would have had the *courage of Lohmann*? I'm lucky to be a Jew so I didn't have to *make that choice.*"

(Stops herself, suddenly realizing she has gone too far and her intensity has become overwhelming.)

Aahh. When I try to tell his stories I begin to hyperventilate or something. Do you hear that? I keep inhaling and I don't exhale, something like that. I can't tell you his stories. I don't have any filter for them. Or maybe the opposite is true. They're full of myth. I can hear the myth and the awe creep into my voice and it makes me feel sick because I don't know what that has to do with him? You should go to Lansing and meet him. He'll cook you dinner. I am so not kidding, he'll cook all of you dinner. You'll have to stay up really late because they eat at around eleven o'clock or midnight, but both of my parents would tell you these stories. Incredible stories! And then after dinner, if you want, my mother will take you to see Meijer's Thrifty Acres. It's incredible. It's like the showplace of Lansing. It's one store, not a mall, but one store where you can buy anything, you could buy anything at Meijer's Thrifty Acres! You could buy a loaf of bread, you could buy a bra, you could buy an above-ground pool there if you wanted to! You could buy a gun. It's incredible! It's open twenty-four hours.

(The sound of a slide interrupts her and she runs upstage to describe the following onslaught of blank images.)

This is one of the extra-wide parking spaces at Meijer's. It's one of my mother's favorite things about the store. *(The slide changes)* This is a picture of my dad on a roller coaster. *(The slide changes)* This is a picture of my mom and dad having dinner at the Olive Garden at the mall which is directly across Saginaw highway from Meijer's. *(The slide changes)* This is a picture of my dad getting his insulin shot. *(The slide changes)* This is a picture of me not being able to hold his world in my head. *(The slide changes)* This is a picture of my father's funeral—which is odd because my father's still alive. *(The slide changes)* This is a picture of my hands. And here you can see I'm holding my grandmother and my grandfather and his students from the Jewish school and the chairs that they sat in and the streets that they walked on and the way they held a pen and the funniest joke they ever told and their particular Jewish German accent and the things that made them cry, and all these things have slipped through my fingers because <u>I couldn't remember any of it.</u>

(The sound of one final slide click. Then we hear the sound of crickets. The woman picks up a cigarette from the stool and takes a drag and, in doing so, takes on the persona of her father. She goes to the chair, moves it into a square of light center stage and sits down. It is nighttime.)

During the Second World War, Lisa, I was working as an army interrogator and one of the prisoners who was assigned to me for interrogation had acknowledged having worked with the Gestapo. He held an S.S. rank usually reserved for Gestapo agents, but he insisted he had been only a driver. This seemed a little strange but he was very self-possessed and I could make no real dent in his preposterous story. So, I sent him back to camp—not to his regular barracks but to solitary confinement. Every two

29

or three days I had him returned to me. Each of these interrogations took only five or ten minutes, but every time I sent him back to his cell I had his conditions made a little more severe. His food rations were reduced. His window was boarded up. His blankets were taken away. And on the morning of his last interrogation, he was obviously tired and not as sharp as usual. I started with the routine questions and got the routine answers. Then I asked him if he'd ever made any arrests in the Kraków Ghetto and he said no. I asked him if he had ever driven a car inside the Ghetto and he said yes. So I asked him if he thought it was a lot of fun to go joyriding inside the Ghetto and, of course, he said no. So I said, "Then you did participate in arrests?" And, for some reason, this time this crazy Marx Brothers' routine worked, and he said yes. And when it came to him what he had said, he admitted that he had been a Gestapo agent. And then he broke down and he cried. And then the dam burst. And he said:

(Leaning forward.)

"I can't stand it. I can't live like this anymore. I never thought I did anything wrong and now everyone is telling me I'm a criminal. I was fourteen when my father joined the Nazi party. I grew up believing this movement was the salvation of the German people. I wanted to be a patriotic German and a good and moral human being and now you and those like you come and tell me that everything I thought was good and moral and patriotic was, in fact, evil. And the things I was told were destructive and treasonous and evil, were really good and proper. So here I am, at the age of thirty-two, and I have an ulcer and I hurt and I'm being told that if only I'd done my job badly there might be some hope for me, and I can't live like that," he said, "and I can't accept that."

(Leaning back.)

I looked across my desk at this man, and I knew he could have been me. If I hadn't had the "good fortune" of being born a Jew, I might well have been sitting where he was sitting and saying the things he was saying. I, too, am capable of becoming enamored of ideas or ideologies. I, too, can take refuge, if I need it, in the saying, "You can't make an omelette without breaking eggs." So there he sat, this Gestapo agent, across the table from me, and I knew how very much alike we were and that he, in a very real sense, was my brother. And I felt very close to him.

And then I had to decide what to do with this man whom I thought of as a brother. And I said to myself, Well, it doesn't really much matter what he believed. We're all responsible for our actions. And I ordered him turned over to the Polish liaison officer. I knew what would probably happen to him because the communist officers had indicated they would take him on the train as far as we would pay the railroad fare, and when they crossed the border, they would take him off the train, make him dig a hole, and shoot him into it. I'm not entirely certain that that's what happened, but I think it likely. I think it likely that I sent this man whom I thought of at that moment as a brother to be killed after digging his own grave.

(Stands.)

The park is closing in ten minutes. *(She returns the chair to its place and sits)* We split up a little at the end so that some of us can ride the Mantis, a new stand-up roller coaster, and some of us can get one last batch of Cedar Point fries and maybe a shake for the ride home and maybe some . . . fudge. The caravan of cars is parked right by the gate, in the handi-capped zone, of course, and then we've all made it back except for Dad and Aunt Kitty. I've reached my family-day limit and I am ready to go. "Buckle your seat belts," I say to Peg and Mary, "they'll be here in a minute." And we wait. "Let's go, go, go," I say. And we wait some more. Finally they wander into the headlights of the cars. Peg says, "Oh my God, Lisa. Your dad doesn't look so good." "He's okay," I say. Peg says he looks a little green. Their walk out of the front gates of Cedar Point to the front seat of the car is torturously slow. Peg and Mary watch intently and send Catholic prayers with every step. I slump in the back seat and mutter impa-tiently: "He's fine."

About six months later Dad has triple bypass surgery. Somebody, he or my mom, casually mentions that he thinks he probably had a little heart attack on the way out of Cedar Point last summer. Peg says she is not going to Cedar Point with my family again. "You people are insane!" she says. My mother always says, "You know the doctors told us that your grandmother was near death at least a hundred times and she turned out to be fine. Well, okay, eventually she did die, but that was the exception, not the rule."

(Stands.)

At the end of the day I'm feeling giddy, almost euphoric. We've done it. It's over. Check. Dad says, "Where is my bag of glasses?" And I say, "I'm sure they're in the car. I must have left them in the car, Dad. I know they're in the car." They're not in the car and now it's nearly dark. We can't leave without them. Dad says it's all right but his face is ashen.

(A breathless, nervous sax solo begins to play, underscoring the rest of this section.)

Elizabeth talks to the guard in German. He says we can drive in, along the railroad tracks. It's pitch dark. We drive to the end of the tracks. Now there's Auschwitz dirt on Elizabeth's car. We leave Dad in the car and take two little flashlights to look on the monument where I'd changed film in the camera. I have to be careful and look where I'm going so that I don't fall into the ruins of the gas chambers. Elizabeth has lost her mind. She's racing all over the monument and screaming. "I don't see them. Do you see them, Lisa? Oh, God, oh, God, I don't see them. Are they here? Do you see them?" We get back in the car. We drive back to the front gate. The other place I could have left them was in the barracks. I had stopped to take pictures in the barracks where there was writing on the rafters in old German script that said things like: "One louse and you're dead. Honesty endures longest. Cleanliness is healthiness." We can't drive the car over the tracks. So I go with the guard on foot to look. He's taking me into all the barracks. There are a hundred or so. He speaks a little German. I speak none but I manage to put together the sentence, "Barrack mit schreiben." He takes me right to the barracks with the writing. I have to run to keep up with him. When he gets too far ahead I'm in pitch dark. How does this man work here? All day the air has smelled like smoke and we've heard dogs barking in the distance. My dad says that Jews and dogs don't get along. I've never in my whole life been so frightened.

The glasses are not here. We'll find them the next day at the visitor's center but tonight we don't know that and we're feeling broken. We thought we could walk away from this.

I can't bear that there's a piece of us left here somewhere. I know that my dad has lost much more important things than his glasses in this place, but that was a long time ago. I have an image now that he has a bubble around his life that's complete and apart from this place and now I've broken the circle and lost a piece of him here.

(Music fades out.)

I thought I could come here for a day and then get on with my life and now we have to come back here in the morning.

(Sax music moves her to the wedding area and fades out as she begins to speak.)

My mother has begun to prepare for the wedding. She's had her hair cut and styled. This is something she hasn't done in thirty years. She's never worn makeup but she's asked me to hire a professional makeup person to do her face the day of the wedding. This is an unprecedented amount of money for my mother to spend on herself but she's got it all figured out. She's telling everyone, "Listen, I'm going to make this last. When they're done with me I'm going to have my face shellacked." The other thing is that she's started buying all these dresses. Now my mother has been wearing the same style of Sears catalog housedress since 1963. But now she's buying dresses by the bagload and bringing them home to try on for my father, whose opinion is a little suspect, as you can imagine.

But on the day of the wedding none of us can take our eyes off her. She looks so beautiful. My brother and my aunts are really glad to get pictures. "I hate to say this," David says, "but at least when she's gone we'll have some photos." But you know, I don't think the pictures look like her. She doesn't look like a photograph to me. I think that must be it. I think we must learn over time to make the translation from live person to still photo and I never did that with my mother. I see her in my mind. She looks like a laughing girl.

(Crosses back to center.)

So we went to this wedding. I didn't even buy new panty hose. I just put on some old dress from the back of the closet and Peggy dug something up, and off we went to the Seaview Jewish Center in Canarsie. Shoshi had asked us to come early to help her get dressed. Because we're in the theater. And so we know something about costumes.

The Seaview Jewish Center sports a wonderful design out of a 1972 James Bond movie with mirror sculptures on the walls and little fountains in the corners with colored lights that dance and shimmer when you plug the brown cord into the eye-level wall socket just to the left. The floors are peel-and-stick parquet and the rooms are separated with those big motorized accordion partitions which run on tracks in the floor. You know the kind of partitions—the kind that, it was always rumored, had crushed a child to death in gym class. Peg and I went into the "bride's room," as instructed, and there was Shoshi surrounded by women in pastel lace dresses having her makeup done by an Orthodox woman with one of those turbany scarfy hats covering her hair. Shoshi pointed to me and Peg and said, "Everybody, I want you to meet my two new sisters!" And all the women turned to look at us and the makeup lady said, "Really? Wow! You two don't look like sisters at all!" And we said, "No, we're not sisters. We're . . . We're . . . You know . . ." What? Really, what? Girlfriends? Too insubstantial. "Spouse" might have been a good word but I got afraid it was too strong. I had a horrible vision that if I said the word "spouse" these women's heads would explode leaving a tattered charcoaly ball sitting on their necks. And so I said, "We're partners." And the women went, "Oh . . . oh . . ." And I could see them thinking, Partners in what?

For some reason it made me think of the time Peg and I went camping down South. Peg got really frustrated with me during the trip because the whole time we were in the South I kept repeating over and over, "Those two girls were kissin' so I had to kill 'em."

(Crosses to stand behind the chair.)

My parents had a small wedding. My mother didn't let anyone come except her mother and her best friend. She says, "Well, I don't know what else I was supposed to do. I didn't expect your father to show up." The way my father tells the story, on the day of their wedding he put on a suit and he put his laundry in the backseat of the car and thought to himself, Well, either I'll get married or I'll go to Ohio and do my laundry. He told me once that he married her for her walk. He told me another time that he married her because she's a person who acts morally rather than one who thinks about what kind of acts are moral—which is what he thinks he does.

(Crosses back to center.)

My mother had planned for the day after David and Shoshi's wedding what she called a postmortem, which was basically a get-together in which all the members of our family would gather for the purpose of making fun of the wedding. But an unexpected thing happened at my brother's wedding. I became enchanted. We all became enchanted by this wedding. When the lights came on, I had never seen any place as beautiful as the Seaview Jewish Center in Canarsie. And when the band began to play I danced and my cousins danced and Peg twirled my aunt around in her wheelchair, and during the dinner Peg got everyone at our table whipped up into a frenzy yelling: "Table twelve rules the wedding!" And everyone got so excited! And this guy that I grew up with turned to me and said, "Peg is incredible." And I said, "Well, yes, she's got that Irish Catholic camp counselor thing going." And he said, "Well it really works. I mean for just a second I found myself thinking, I think table twelve is the best."

And during the service, when my parents walked my brother in and stood with him under the Chupah . . . I cried.

You know, a couple of years ago I went to see the movie, *Little Women*. And it was in a big theater and there were only about thirty people there and they were all women and we were all sitting separately, scattered about in this huge theater. And when Beth dies, all the women in the theater started to cry, but it wasn't the usual quiet sniffling you hear sometimes in a theater. These women were racked with sobs. All around me I could hear noises like— *(Makes huge, hiccupping, wailing, crying noises)*

And that's how I was crying at my brother's wedding.

It had never dawned on me in a million years that I would feel anything other than a big, judgey reaction to the whole thing. But, when I saw my father standing there all I could see was the soul in this little old man who'd lost his mother and his father and his country and his culture and it's all gone forever and this was the closest he was ever going to come to it again and it didn't feel like enough and it felt like too much for me, and so I cried and then I made everyone sitting around me take an oath that they hadn't seen me doing it because I can't be going around crying at weddings.

(A slide clicks onto the scrim. The woman turns around to look at it. Then she turns back to the audience.)

I have a checklist in my head: things I have to do before my father dies. Number one: look him in the eye and tell him that

I love him. Okay. I did that. Check. Number two: go with him to see the place where his parents were killed. Okay. I did that. Check. Number three: make this video about his life. I've been trying to look at the videotape. It's excruciating. Peg and Mary and I are taping him in his study, at his office, in the park. We say, "Can you show us about your glasses? Great, that was really good. Can you tell us the story about saying good-bye to your parents? Great, great. You know what? That was really, really good. Can you tell it to us again but make it a little more concise? Stop, stop. Hold on. A truck is going by. Hold on. Okay, can you say that again?"

There he is in front of the camera all by himself trying so hard.

"Stop," we say, "can you say that again?"

(Looks back at the slide for a moment, then turns back to the audience.)

He's lived in Michigan for forty years. He eats in front of the TV. He takes a cardiac fitness class at the community college. His life in Lansing is like a translucent overlay that doesn't quite match up. The edges are blurred.

Then we got to Germany and my father was home. Friends picked us up and it felt as if they cared for us like we were little babies. They fed us and they gave us feather beds to sleep in and they drove us wherever we needed to go, and my father was home. He's in focus here, I thought. He's in context.

(Turns back to look at the slide and utters a small gasp as if seeing it anew. She quietly describes what she sees.)

My father is a small man, contained and neat. He smells like lavender. He's wearing a suit.

(Turns back to the audience.)

I tried to imagine seeing my grandparents and I had a fantasy I would see them in Meijer's Thrifty Acres. They'd be hovering over the frozen foods section. It's so cold there. They'd be at a thirty-degree angle. Bobbing a little. A small smile on their lips. They'd be arm in arm. In my fantasy I ask my grandparents if they want to see my father. I pluck them out of the air and sit them gently in the car—the big, American Oldsmobile. I take them to his office. I carry them inside. "Wait here," I say. I knock on my father's door. "Dad, there's someone here to see you!" "What?" he says. He's seventy-five years old. He's hard of hearing. "Wait here." I bring them in. They see him. "Valter," they say.

He can't tell who they are. When he looks at their heads, he sees only flowers.

When I was in college I was taught that if you are standing near a piece of furniture on stage you should put your hand on it because that will make you look bigger.

(Crosses to the chair. Puts her hand on it.)

See? See how that works?

(Her hand drops and then she slowly replaces it.)

I'm putting my hand on my father's life.

(Lights fade to black.)

End of Play

101
Humiliating
Stories

Production History

The script for *101 Humiliating Stories* was developed at Dixon Place, New York Theatre Workshop and Downtown Art Company, and was further developed through collaboration with Jamie Leo.

101 Humiliating Stories premiered at Performance Space 122 in January 1993, under the direction of Jamie Leo. The set and sound were designed by Jamie Leo, the lights by Tye Burris, the costume by Susan Wild and the technical manager was Diana Arecco.

A slightly modified version of the play (which appears here) was presented at Serious Fun! at Lincoln Center on July 29, 1993, under the direction of John Robert Hoffman. The set was designed by Amy Shock, the lights by Lori E. Seid, the costume by Chip White and Jose Gutierrez and the production stage manager was Lori E. Seid.

Production Notes

A note on performance.

The first thing Jamie Leo [director of first production] said to me about this piece was, "You can't just talk about humiliation in the past tense. We have to see you actually being humiliated." And so we developed a series of moments where things go wrong, either because of something external—like a phone call or papers falling off a music stand—or because of some internal failure—like sudden anxiety over how the audience will feel when they realize there aren't really 101 humiliating stories, or an overpowering urge to sleep. Each one of these breaks is meant to feel completely real, like a horrible mistake that should make the audience feel, for a moment, as if they're watching a theatrical car crash. The running device of checking in with the audience should have a tone of utter sincerity and, to this end, these interactions are slightly improvisational. Additional check-ins may be added as necessary.

Setting.

Stage right is a pleasantly decorative straight-backed chair and a side table upon which rests a lamp, a telephone, a lipstick and a powder compact. Tucked slightly behind the chair is a kitchen stool, the kind from the 1950s, made of painted metal with a back and steps, which fold out. Mid-stage left and slightly upstage is a music stand on which rests an unbound script. Downstage far left is a podium which is used for the graduation speeches. There is a black scrim across the back of the playing area, and a platform behind it.

A mashed version of Mendelssohn's "In the Spring" plays. Lights fade up revealing the figure of a woman running in slow motion behind the scrim. She is on the platform, so appears to be floating. As she runs, she speaks. This first story is delivered in a slightly overblown, full-voiced, declamatory style.

The year is 1975. A young unnamed midwestern girl (of Jewish descent) runs back and forth across the playing field behind her junior high school. It is gym class. It is the track segment. The girl is wearing a green and white striped polyester gym suit. Green is not her color. It is not anyone's color, but it is particularly disturbing on this girl. She has long hair—long 1970s junior high hair with a center part (known in the 1990s as "the dreaded center part").

(Stops running. There is a long and indecisive pause during which the music continues, making it appear as though she has lost her place. As she says the following, she fumbles her way out from behind the scrim onto the stage and then out into the house, heading toward the tech booth.)

(To the sound operator) Janet? Janet? Janet? Janet? Janet? Janet? Can you turn the sound off for just a second? *(The volume goes up)* No, off! Cut it. Can you just cut it for a second. Yeah. And then we'll come back to it, but if you could just cut it . . . *(Music stops)* Thanks. Could I have some lights? Thanks. *(Speaking with utter sincerity to the audience members, among whom she is now standing)* I'm sorry. I just wanted to say, before we go on, that I know that these stories can be very evocative for

people. And I know that the junior high segments in particular can be very resonant. And I want to be responsible to that—as an artist—and not bring up a lot of feelings and then send you back out into the world with a lot of things unresolved. And so, you know what? I can check in periodically to make sure you're all doing okay. And if you have feelings that come up during the show that you would like to talk about, I want you to feel free to raise your hand and I think everyone here would feel fine about focusing on *(Speaking to one person in the audience)* you for a second . . . I'm sorry, not you in particular. I don't mean to suggest you have deeper psychological problems than anyone else here . . . but . . . I mean, maybe you do, I don't know. No, I'm sure you're fine. You're fine. *(Back to the larger group)* So, we'll focus in and then, when you're feeling better we can go on. Okay? So is everyone okay so far? Okay? Okay. All right, Janet, let's continue.

(Returns to the stage, starts to head back behind the scrim and then changes her mind and remains center stage.)

It's probably better for me to be out here, stay a little bit more . . . connected. Where was I . . . *(Mumbles quickly through the beginning speech until she remembers where she left off)* Ah! Okay, Janet, let's continue. *(Music resumes. She switches back into overblown style)* The gym suit does not fit her well. It doesn't fit anyone well except for Tricia Pickett. *(She indulges a tiny reverie)* Tricia Pickett . . . *(She snaps out of it)* But on *this* girl, the gym suit is tight across the butt and bust, and the elastic hits her a few inches below her waist giving her a permanent wedgie which she must constantly and inconspicuously try to adjust without using her hands. With the gym suit she wears knee highs—navy blue, nerdy knee highs—which she keeps up with rubber bands. She tells herself that no one looks good in gym class. There is an illusion of anonymity in numbers. The girl holds her breath and runs back and forth, back and forth.

On the way back to the locker room she begins to feel confused. Where is my locker? she wonders. What is my combination? She goes into the gym office to ask. What she says is, "Ms. Roper, hello. I'm going to pass out." This is as surprising to her as it is to Ms. Roper. Ms. Roper gives the girl a wastebasket and goes to get help. Ms. Roper's idea of help is Jan the Narc. Ms. Roper thinks the girl is on drugs. The girl would probably be having a much better time in junior high school if she were on drugs. Then she would know better than to follow Jan who takes the girl out of the locker room and into the hall . . . Into the hall where one never, never ventures in a gym suit. Luckily, it is between classes. The girl will go to the clinic. They'll call her mother. But the girl starts to get dizzier and dizzier. She begins to lean heavily, overwhelming Jan who is the size of a jockey. Please Jan. You're tough! You're a narc, Jan! Get her to the clinic, Jan! Heave her over your shoulder and, for the love of God, get her to the clinic before the bell rings! Jan lets the girl slip to the floor.

(Accompanied by hallucinatory, slo-mo light and sound effects, she falls to the floor in agonized slow motion, complete with silent, open-mouthed screaming and a slowed-down impact bounce at the end.)

The girl lays there. And yes, the bell rings. Jan does not help the girl up but finds it more efficient to let her lie there for a full five minutes until the hall is clear again. The story is true. The girl has never recovered.

(Unceremoniously gets up and crosses to chair and table to reapply her lipstick.)

I just have to take a minute here to freshen . . . and check . . . Sometimes in the exertion of that first piece, in some of the more complicated dance movement, I get a little bit of a clowny face, you know, a little bit of a lipstick goatee. And I like to brighten a little before I go on. *(Applies lipstick)* And I like to just check for any damage. It's a little hard since the mirror is a little small and I can only see my face a piece at a time. *(Moves the mirror to inspect her face in sections)* I have to put it all together in my head later. *(Applies powder)* A little powder so that I don't fade too early. It'll happen eventually but . . . It's a good color, right? The lipstick? It took me a long time to find the perfect color because for a long time I didn't know what I obviously know now . . . that I'm an autumn.

(The sound of birds chirping. This is actually the phone ringing, which becomes apparent when she answers it.)

Hello? Yes, this is Lisa . . . Kron, I pronounce it Krōn, actually. *(Gives the audience an "I'll be with you in one sec" gesture)* Debby Downs . . . from my high school. Sure I remember you. *(Makes a face to the audience indicating she has no recollection of Debby Downs)* Really? Well, yes, I guess it is about that time, but you know, Debby, I'm really very busy so I don't think I'll be able to attend . . . Really? Well, Debby, what an interesting idea. I'm very flattered, but you know, Debby, I don't think I'm probably the right person for that. I don't actually do "skits." Yeah, well, Debby, I still don't think I'm probably the right person for that. Why? Um . . . Well, Debby . . . because, uh . . . Well, because I'm a big lesbian, actually, is the reason. So I don't think it would be such a good idea. Probably you should get a magician or something for that. Well, all right, we can talk about it. But can we talk later? Because I've got an audience here. Great. All right, let me get your number. Hold on. Let me get a pen. *(To audience)* Does anyone have a pen I could borrow? *(Gets a pen from someone in the audience)* Thanks. I'll get it back to you. *(Gets a scrap of paper from the music stand. Returns to the phone)* Okay, Debby. Deb? *(Pause)* Hi, De . . . Yeah, that *Little Mermaid* is cute, the kids like that . . . Okay, let me get this number. 517, of course, *(Mumbles the rest)*. Okay, Debby, I'll call you back later tonight. How late can I call? 9:30. Okay. That's going to be a little early for me. Can I call you tomorrow? Okay, great, I'll give you a call tomorrow then. 'Bye . . . yes, it was good talking to you too. 'Bye . . . Okay, well, if you run into her again you tell her I said hello. *(Doing the I'm-trying-to-hang-up-but-the-other-person-keeps-talking bob)* Okay, 'bye. 'Bye. 'Bye. 'Bye. 'Bye. 'Bye. 'Bye. 'Bye. *(Hangs up)*

Where was I? . . . Oh, yes. I'm an autumn . . .

(Bird-chirping phone rings again.)

Hello. Hi, Mom. Yes, she did, she just called me. No, that's all right. No, I don't think I'm going to do it. Because I don't think my work is really appropriate for that. I don't think they are really hoping for a lesbian performance artist. Can we talk later because I've got some people here? Okay, Mom, we've been over this before. I don't think my work is explicit. There's a difference between being a lesbian and being explicit. I'm a lesbian, I say I'm a lesbian. I have a girlfriend. I say things like . . . I went to the store with my girlfriend. I don't think that's being explicit. Can we talk later? Okay. I love you too. 'Bye.

Where was I? Oh, yes, I'm an autumn. So I first discovered I'm an autumn a few years ago when I was working one of my many temp jobs, and on this particular job, in addition to my usual duties as a word processor, one of the things I had to do was to run errands. And on this particular day I was to run an errand to the bank to cash a petty cash check and then come right back to work. And I went to the bank and cashed a check for a couple of hundred dollars, and on the way back to work I was doing this thing that I like to do of checking out my reflection in store windows. Because I think this is the only way to correctly assess the way you look to other people. Because you know that if you look at yourself in your mirror at home you know the way to arrange yourself so that you get the most flattering appearance. Like, if I turn by body this way I'll have a more slender profile and if I tilt my head this way the light will hit me in a more flattering way, and you look in the mirror *(Looks in an imaginary mirror, standing in a completely contorted position)* and you think, I look pretty good. But if you really want to know how you look to other people you have to do that completely brutal thing of checking out your reflection as you walk down the street in store windows. And so I was walking along Seventh Avenue and looking into the store windows and I have to say that I was very disturbed by what I saw because what I saw was a person who had no outlines to her body. I had no definition to me. I was like an amorphous blob. I was like a scoop of mashed potatoes walking down the street. And the worst part was that I had no facial features. Does that ever happen to you? I just had eye sockets. I was like a bad haircut with eye sockets. And I thought, This is not what I want to see when I look at my reflection. I want to see a cohesive visual image. And I was inspired thinking about my friend Chris who is always a cohesive visual image. And the key to the way Chris looks is her lipstick. Chris is the kind of woman who has been wearing lipstick since she was five years old. She's the kind of woman whose worn so much lipstick that even when she doesn't have lipstick on she still has lipstick on. Do you know what I mean? She has like a lipstick residue. She has like a lipstick reservoir which goes from her lips through to the back of her head. And I thought, I want to be like that. And Chris always bought her lipstick at the Prescriptives counter. And I was right outside Macy's so I thought, I'm going to go in there and get myself a Prescriptives lipstick.

Now, up until this time, I had always bought my make-up at the Woolworths. And you know, when you go to the Woolworths you shop in your own private, personal little world. No one talks to you in the Woolworths. And there are seven thousand lipsticks there and they are all 99¢. And they all have clear plastic caps and so you pick a lipstick and you take a mirror, that's also for sale, and you hold it up and say to yourself, Would this look good on me, or would this look gaggy? And I never knew. And I could never even narrow it down, because, of course at that time, I didn't know that I'm an autumn.

In any case, I went into the Macy's and I was looking at the lipsticks when out of the corner of my eye I saw a woman who had big hair, and she was wearing a white lab coat and she had what my friend Mary Beth calls a Shroud of Turin face. Because she was wearing so much makeup that if she were to lay her face down on a white pillowcase it would leave a ghostly mirror image of her face behind. And she said to me, "Can I help you?" And I said, "No, thank you, I'm in my own personal, private world." And she said, "Do you know your color group?" And I said, "No." And she said, "Would you like a color group test?" And I said, "Yes." And I don't know why I said yes. Except that it sounded like something I would need, like a Pap smear and, like a Pap smear, I didn't think it would take too long so I could get right back to work because, remember, they were waiting for the petty cash.

She was joined by two other big-haired, lab-coated, Shroud of Turin-faced women and they sat me down in a chair and they started to work on me. *(Brings the stool downstage and sits)* And the first thing they did was to start cleaning me off with astringent. They had, like, bales of cotton and buckets of astringent and they cleaned me off all over. And then they started to put things on me. And the first thing the first woman put on me was foundation and then she

handed me the mirror and said, "How does this look?" And
I looked and the other two looked and they said, "This is
incredible. You look GORGEOUS. When you came in here
you were like a dead thing. Now your skin, it's like porcelain!
It's unbelievable how you look." And it was unbelievable how
I looked. Then the first one put on eyeliner and eye shadow
and mascara and she held up the mirror and she said, "How
does that look?" And the other two looked, and they said,
"This is incredible. Your eyes are just popping out of your
head. They're huge! They're huge!" And I looked and my
eyes were huge. I was like some kind of a Bambi thing. Then
the first one put on lip liner and lip color and cheek color and
said, "How does this look?" And she looked, and the other
two looked, and I looked and all together we began to scream
about how gorgeous I was and there was pandemonium in
this corner of the store over how incredibly gorgeous I
looked. Then they put all these things out on the counter.
Now we had the astringent, the foundation, the eyeliner, the
lip liner, the lip color, the powder, the eye shadow and the
blusher. And the lady said, "Which one of these things would
you like to take home with you today?" And I said, "I have
to have all of those things." And I didn't have any idea how
much those things cost and I didn't even ask. I just handed
them my Visa card the way people on credit card commer-
cials charge an entire ski vacation. And this was three weeks
before Macy's started to take anything but a Macy's card.
And she said, "I'm so sorry, we don't take the Visa card." And
I said, "Fine." And I reached into my bag. And I took out an
envelope. And I handed them all two hundred dollars of
petty cash from my office. And then I took my little bag. And
I walked back to work. And on my way back I thought to
myself, "Hmm. I hope they don't notice how much more
beautiful I am." And I thought of all the reasons I might have
been at the bank cashing a petty cash check for three hours
and forty-five minutes. And I got back to work. And I looked

at them. And they looked at me. And I said, "I've just spent all the petty cash on makeup."

(A long, indecisive pause which ends with the following confession:)

I don't really have 101 humiliating stories. I have about seventeen humiliating stories. But within each story there are several humiliations which, depending how you count, could add up to 101. So I just wanted to clear that up right now because after the show I didn't want you thinking, Well, she was really funny, but there weren't 101 humiliating stories. I don't want you obsessing about that. So let's just let that expectation go. All right? Let's just let it float up to the ceiling. Okay.

(Pops into an enthusiastic, a cappella rendition of the theme from Entertainment Tonight *and crosses center.)*

This is a section called "Geeky Celebrity Encounters." I have three celebrity encounters, the first two of which, I believe, lead inextricably to the third, which is an encounter I had with Sigourney Weaver.

Celebrity Encounter Number 1:
My first celebrity encounter was with Howard Lancour, who, as some of you probably know, was the anchorman from WJIM-TV in Lansing, Michigan. This actually was before Howard Lancour became anchorman at WJIM and while he was still Mr. Mayor, the human host of the *Alley Kat and Pansy* show . . . (You know, I love the phrase "human host" because it makes it sound like Alley Kat and Pansy are going to burst out of his stomach . . .) Anyway . . . On my sixth birthday it was arranged that, along with my entire first grade class, I would be seated in the gallery of children on bleachers who appeared on the *Alley Kat and Pansy* show. Now, Alley Kat and

Pansy were two lively puppet characters that spoke to us from over a picket fence. You know, they say that celebrities often look different in person—a little shorter, a little older, a little thinner—Alley Kat and Pansy had never been dry cleaned. They had been thrown in the washer and thrown in the dryer and they had that kind of wear and tear. They were decrepit. They were moth-eaten and decrepit. I remember Pansy in particular having a stomach-turning effect on me. One of his eyes was a little loose and hanging by a thread. And what was even worse was . . . You know they talked to us from over this picket fence. And watching on TV there was the happy, backyard world of the picket fence. But in the studio there was a piece of picket fence that ended here and ended here *(Indicates about a four-foot width)* and on either side there were two old men's butts sticking out. And I could not deal with this. So I turned my attention to the giant slow-poke sucker I had been given as were all birthday children on the *Alley Kat and Pansy* show. Do you remember giant slow-poke suckers? This sucker was six inches wide by two feet long. And I had never seen a piece of candy this big. My brother and I weren't even allowed to chew gum. And I just wanted to see what it looked like. So I started to take it out of the box, and I guess when I did I must have crinkled the paper a little because as I was trying to take it out, Mr. Mayor aborted his cartoon introduction. I think he was introducing *Tennessee Tuxedo* and he stopped right in the middle and he said, "Little girl. Don't eat that now." Which I experienced as, "PUT DOWN THAT GODDAMN SUCKER!"

Celebrity Encounter Number 2:
When I was in college I studied theater in London for a semester . . . as you can tell. One day, attending a play in the West End, I realized during the interval that the man sitting in front of me was Derek Jacobi, whom I considered, and whom I had often referred to as, the God of acting for his

portrayal of Claudius in the PBS series. I knew I must make some connection with this man. So, all through the second act I positioned my leg so that when he threw his head back in laughter it would bump on my knee. And when the play was over, I timed my exit from my row with his so that when I reached the aisle he would be directly behind me. This required a good deal of shoving of the people in my row, but I felt it was necessary. And as we left the theater I walked at a highly erratic pace so that he would be forced to trip on my heels. My personal triumph is that I'm pretty sure he, Derek Jacobi, found me to be a total irritation.

And this brings us to our third encounter which, as I have said, is an encounter I had with Sigourney Weaver. Several years ago, my girlfriend Peggy and I attended a party for Lambda Legal Defense, one of the hosts of which was Sigourney Weaver. Now, this was right after the *Alien* movies had come out and my girlfriend was in love with Sigourney Weaver. Her love for Sigourney Weaver was second only to her love for Linda Hamilton in the *Terminator* movies—so you get the genre. And everyone knew this and they all came up to us and said, "Would you like to meet Sigourney Weaver?" And we said, "No, that sounds like the makings of a geeky celebrity encounter. We'll just stand here in the corner and stare at her for a few minutes and that will be fine." Well, a little later in the party, I don't know what got into me, but I looked over and saw that Sigourney Weaver was deep in conversation with Liz Smith. And Peggy and I knew the photographer, Tom. And I said, "Tom, Peggy and I are going to go over and stand with our backs to Sigourney Weaver and Liz Smith and we're going to act like we're snubbing them. And you take our picture." They were deep in conversation and they didn't even notice we were there, and we stood with our backs to them and did this: *(Looks over her shoulder with an expression of total disdain)*. And Tom took the picture. And as soon as he did he said, "Miss Weaver, these two young ladies would like to have their picture taken with you . . . They're actresses too!" Well, it was horrifying, it was completely humiliating. And I don't know why I did this, I think I was trying to lighten things up a little, to inject a little humor into the situation, I don't know why I did it, but as soon as the flash went off, there was that explosion of light and I turned to Sigourney Weaver and I screamed at her, "DON'T ASK ME FOR MY PICTURE AGAIN!" She was very gracious. She didn't know what I'd said, she just knew that this woman started to scream at her. She was very nice. She walked away. *(Backs up, hands up defensively, muttering a bewildered pleasantry)* You could see that in her mind she was going, John Hinckley, John Hinckley, John Hinckley, John Hinckley.

We have this picture hanging in our home. In the picture Sigourney Weaver is standing to one side—tall, she's so tall, beautiful, she's so beautiful—looking out at the camera. Peggy is on the other side, looking down, a little embarrassed but still very attractive. And I am in the middle. Looking up at Sigourney Weaver like this: *(Poses looking straight up, frozen in a manic, open-mouthed smile)*

(Notices the pen from the audience member still sitting on the table) Oh my God, I forgot to give this back to you. I'm so sorry. Were you thinking about it? Sorry.

(Crosses to the phone and dials) Hi Hazel. How are you? Good. Is Peg there? Thanks. *(Pause)* Hi Hon. How are you. Everything's okay? Good. Good. Yes, it's going well. *(Referring to the audience)* They're very nice. There are a lot of them! Yeah . . . Yes, actually, I did want to tell you this one thing that happened. This woman called me from my high school, Debby Downs, she wants me to come home and perform at my high school reunion. No, I'm not going to do it. Yeah, but it sounds like a big setup, don't you think. Yeah, but I'm a big lesbian. Well, I don't know, do you want to come with me? Oh. Okay, um, listen, I've got an audience here, I have to go. No, I'm not upset. You know, I asked for your

opinion and you gave it, so that's great. I have to go. 'Bye.
(Hangs up)

You know, I worked as an office temp for many years and
sometimes I came out on my jobs, but most of the time
I didn't and I always felt really torn about this. I felt like
I should come out but it was always a little awkward. I was
never at these places for very long and who was I going to
come out to anyway? I wasn't working for those people, I was
working for my agency. I was out at my agency. They were
all lesbians too. Anyway, I was always torn about this and at
some point I got the first full-time job I had had in a long
time, working as a word processor in a midtown corporate
law firm. And I got this job the same time some other things
were happening in the world. The Thomas/Hill hearings
were happening and I went to a ten year memorial service for
GMHC at St. John the Divine and these things were working in my brain and reminding me that we don't come out of
the closet to make some esoteric political statement, we come
out for very concrete reasons, to protect ourselves, protect our
lovers, validate our relationships, blah, blah, blah . . . you all
know all this . . . So I thought, you know, I have this opportunity on this job and I'm not going to mess around with this.
I'm going to tell these people that I'm a lesbian. I don't know
what's going to happen. I don't know if they're going to
accept me or reject me. I don't know if they are going to fire
me, but it doesn't matter. I'm just going to do this. I'm just
going to tell these people that I'm a lesbian. And so . . . I
wrote a memo. And as it turns out, these people were great.
They were totally accepting of me. They said, "No problem.
You fit right in here." And when this happened I realized that
I don't really want to fit in at a corporate, midtown law firm.
And I started to do little things to rebel. Although, "rebel-
lious" is probably a little bit of a strong term for what I am.
I'm more contrary, really. And I'd do things like when I
answered the phone, sometimes instead of saying, "word

processing" I'd say, "food processing." And no one ever really noticed, but then when I'd hang up I'd say, "Heh, heh, that was a good one." And the other thing I did was that I didn't dress appropriately for a corporate law firm and this turned out to be a problem. They could deal with the fact that I was a lesbian, but they couldn't deal with the clothes that I was wearing to work, so they called me in to talk to me about it, but they couldn't quite figure out what to say because it wasn't clear to them exactly what the problem was. It was clear I wasn't buying my clothes at Chuckles or Strawberry, like the other secretaries, but beyond that they couldn't quite pin it down. But they wanted to give me something specific so they said to me, "Lisa, we would prefer it if you didn't wear white socks to work . . . because . . . that's important here." And so I started wearing pink socks to work and blue socks and gray socks, which obviously wasn't what they had in mind. Obviously they wanted me to wear panty hose to work but I nipped that right in the bud. I can't remember exactly what I said to them but it was something like, you know, "If I have to wear panty hose to work every day my yeast infection will be on your head." Something like that. They backed off pretty quickly on that. In any case, we reached a sort of uneasy resolution. But after that I always felt a little uncomfortable. When I left my house in the morning I'd feel fine. I'd feel like I was dressed appropriately for an office in the East Village . . . if there is such a thing. But when I'd get to work I'd always feel awkward. It was like that dream that you have where you go to work or you go to school and when you get there you realize you're wearing your pajamas. And I think that was part of the problem. I was just too comfortable. And here were all these women in their tight skirts and their high heels and I looked like I could just take a nap at any time. And I think they resented that a little. Anyway, I always felt a little uncomfortable and so I really began to appreciate the things I do naturally that helped me feel like I fit in with these really very nice people that I was working with. And one of these things was wearing lipstick, because, as you know, I enjoy wearing lipstick. And I began to make a daily ritual out of going into the bathroom and freshening up my lipstick; although this was a little bit of a double-edged sword too because, as any of you who've ever been in a women's room in a corporate office know, there is something about the way the lights are designed in these rooms that highlights the upper-lip hair on a woman. They're all like this. I believe it's part of the patriarchal conspiracy. And so I'd freshen my lipstick and I'd think, "Hmm. Good color, but you're looking a little like Gene Shalit." In any case, this one day in particular, I'd freshened my lipstick, and I was feeling good. Like when I have a little moisturizing color on my lips I fit right in, I'm one of the girls. And I left the bathroom and I was walking back down the hall, back to word processing and I was taking my time and talking to all these very nice people that I worked with, they were such nice people. I stopped and talked with a secretary. She asked about my lipstick. I was like, "Oh, do you like it? I'm an autumn! Prescriptives!" I chatted with a paralegal for a minute. "Nice blouse, Marcy. Where did you get it? Strawberry! It's cute!" I talked with an attorney for a few seconds. He wanted to know if his document was ready. It wasn't ready yet. We had a nice chat. And I got to the door of word processing and one of the secretaries, Pat, came up to me and said, *(Leaning in and whispering)* "Lisa, I have to tell you something." And I said, *(Excited to hear the gossip)* "Yeah?" And she said, "I saw you coming down the hall here . . ." And I said, "Yeah?" And she said, "And I saw you talking to all those people." And I said, "Yeah?" And she said, "And I just wanted to tell you that your skirt is tucked into your tights." "Thanks, Pat."

And I had walked all the way down the long hall sashaying my exposed butt to everyone in the office.

But when I got back into word processing I had kind of an epiphany. And I had to work very hard to control an almost irresistible urge to tuck my skirt back into my tights and take a long walk around the law office. Hello, law office! This is my butt! You don't get a butt like this eating SlimFast for lunch. You have to eat a real lunch to get a butt like this. Welcome to my butt, everyone! Hello Buttville!

(Crosses to graduation podium and delivers the following speech in the self-righteous manner of a lesbian with a big chip on her shoulder.)

Hello everyone, class of 1979, Lansing Everett High School. My name is Lisa Kron and I am a member of the class of 1979. I'd like to thank Debby Downs for asking me here today. Thank you, Debby. I'm very pleased to be here and I'd like to tell you a little about myself. I am a *lesbian*. I work as a solo performance artist in the East Village of NYC. I am here today with my committed partner of five years Peg Healey. She is my *lover*. And she and I are in a theater company together called The Five *Lesbian* Brothers and we're based in the *lesbian* theater collective, the W.O.W. Café. How many people here today are gay or lesbian? *(Looks for raised hands. Sees none)* That's all right. I understand if you don't feel safe in this environment raising your hand. I'd like you straight people here today to know that at least twenty percent of the population is gay or lesbian, so there's a pretty good chance the person sitting next to you could be a gay man or a lesbian. I want you to know that there's at least one lesbian here today. I am a lesbian! And I'm not some deviant they trucked in from New York. I'm from here. I'm from Lansing, Michigan. So there's at least one lesbian here . . . There are two lesbians here! My lover Peggy is here as well. Peggy, raise your hand. *(Pause)* Peg! Raise your hand! Raise it!

(Her focus on bending Peg to her will dissipates and she wanders away from the graduation podium, hovers nowhere for a longish moment, then crosses to the music stand.)

I can't remember what's next.

(Turns the pages of the script looking for her place. A piece of paper flutters to the floor. As she bends to pick it up, she drops part of the sheaf of papers in her hand, and in trying to pick that up, more papers fall. As she struggles to regain order and her composure she mutters the following:)

Oh . . . poop. You know, I have come to accept that I have a whole other set of behaviors that exhibit themselves to the world that I am not aware of. For instance, I am sitting on the couch doing an activity . . . crocheting—one of my hobbies happens to be crocheting. And I think, I am happily crocheting. And everyone else in the room is thinking, She seems so self-conscious and angry and how can she crochet while she is eating compulsively like that?

(Her papers restored, she stands at the music stand.)

I took the bus to high school. Our bus driver was a hippie named Charley who wore the same pair of American flag socks every day and a big animal-fur hat he had obviously crafted himself, probably out of family pets. And every day he fell asleep on the way to school—but just momentarily. We loved our rides to school because we always listened to the same Earth, Wind and Fire tape. *(Earth, Wind and Fire's "That's the Way of the World" begins to play softly)* We loved that tape. There were fifty seats on the bus and seventy-five kids, so each morning it was a mad rush to get on the bus first so that you could get an actual seat and not have to sit on the edge of a seat already occupied by two other kids. Charley never participated in the struggle, but watched us in a half-lidded stupor as seventy-five kids tried to push through a bus door at the same time.

One morning, I had managed to position myself at the front of the pack, gotten up the stairs, was standing at the front, about to make my way down the aisle to one of the coveted seats by the window when I realized that someone was pulling my hair. This was not unusual, actually. It was sort of a daily ritual, in fact, for the person sitting behind me on the bus to pull hairs out of my head one by one. I always looked out the window and pretended I didn't notice.

(Gazes out with a blank-eyed stare while her head is jerked back repeatedly and almost imperceptibly.)

This day, though, my hair was being pulled by a really big hank. I tried to act like I didn't notice, but I wasn't moving anywhere. People were pushing past me and I was pinned to the spot. So I turned to give my torturer one of my finely honed ambiguous looks—this was a look I had developed in which I could confront someone without actually confronting them. I would turn my body toward the person and make no eye contact and try to make my face blank so as not to reveal any angry or about-to-cry emotions and hoped that by just facing this person they would stop doing whatever they were doing to me. But, on this day, when I turned to face this person, I saw that no one was pulling my hair. It had gotten sucked into a little fan Charley had bolted to the ceiling. I gave Charley a look which I hoped would communicate to him that I thought I could arrange to have him paid any amount of money if he would reach into his bag and take out a huge knife and with the same sure-fingered grace he had obviously used to make headgear out of Fido, he would hack off the entire back section of my hair before anyone noticed that I was caught. Charley couldn't deal and he looked through me like I was vapor. Then he started up the bus and drove us to school leaving me to extricate myself, while trying to stay upright around sharp turns in front of a completely rapt audience.

This was the year I had started to think I might someday live down the old-fashioned dress debacle.

As a girl I was devoted to Laura Ingalls Wilder. My friends and I read all of her books over and over again. We loved her descriptions of the beautiful and brutal lives they lived on the frontier. It was because of those books that Patty Rau, Beth Wanders and I begged our mothers to make us "old-fashioned dresses." In calico. Laura Ingalls Wilder always wore calico. And with sunbonnets. We made the terrible mistake of wearing them to school one day, and for the remainder of our time in elementary school traced the moment our ceaseless ostracization began to that day we all went to school dressed like Laura Ingalls Wilder.

(You know, this is an interesting moment in the show for me. Because up until this time I feel like you've been laughing in empathy with me and my humiliations. And at this moment I feel like you're laughing in empathy with my tormentors and looking at me and thinking, "Eew. I would have *hated* her!")

When I was young I loved everything "old-fashioned." I won an honorable mention in Santa's Art Gallery with a picture called "An Old-Fashioned Christmas" It was big, on a wallpaper motif as I recall. The contest was held by WJIM-TV and I went on TV to accept my prize from Santa whom, as a Jew, I knew to be a fraud. And I had to sit on his lap, and all I could think was that my legs were apart over one of his legs and I kept pulling my dress down because I thought the viewing public would be able to look up my dress. I had learned to keep my dress down from Mrs. Hildreth in first grade. Before that time I had not known this was a thing one needed to be concerned about. But one day I was sitting in the reading circle folding my dress up into a neat little roll and Mrs. Hildreth yelled at me to pull my dress down, and so I credit her with teaching me shame.

(Crosses to graduation podium. In this version she is being as polite and positive as she can, but is at an utter loss to describe her life to this audience.)

Hello class of 1979, Lansing Everett High School. I'm very pleased to be here. I'm honored, really, to be here. And I'd like to thank Debby Downs for asking me here. Thank you so much, Debby, really, it's a great honor to be here. I'd like to tell you a little bit about where I've been since I left Lansing Everett, and what I do. I live in New York City and I work as a solo performer, doing one-woman shows, you might say. The kind of theater that I do is . . . well, it's, um, experimental theater, avant-garde theater . . . uh, it's Off-Off-Broadway! actually, is what it is. Um . . . I'm not married. Although I do have a roommate and she's here with me today. She came with me here, uh, because . . . oh, she's always wanted to see Lansing! And, uh, she and I are in a theater company together, actually, The Five Le . . . made up of five women, and we're based in a women's theater collective . . . uh, it's sort of an ensemble, actually . . . a women's ensemble . . . made up of a big, big group of women . . . a big group of women who just like to hang out together, I guess, I don't know what else they'd be doing together . . .

(As the speech self-destructs, she wanders away from the podium, muttering the last lines. She ends up at the stool where she sits.)

I come from the midwest and we don't believe in whining in the midwest. We don't believe in whining, we don't believe in therapy, we don't believe in depression. If you feel bad, it's because of the weather. It's because there's a big barometric pressure zone coming in and when it's gone you'll be fine.

And as a result of being raised in this environment, I don't have any patience for people who whine. For instance, the other day I was in the subway, standing on the platform waiting for the train, and there was a woman standing near me on the platform, near the stairs, and a man ran down the stairs and as he ran by her he stepped on her foot. And when he did, she did this: *(Looks down at foot and then looks up and accusingly yells)* "OW!" I hate that. And the worst thing was that it didn't have anything to do with her foot, right? She didn't go: *(Looks down at foot and cries pitifully)* "Ow." She went: *(Looks up accusingly)* "OW!" I hate that! That's the worst kind of whining. Accusatory whining! And I try to hold myself to this same standard and I try to never be in a position where I will be caught whining.

A few years ago I was working at another one of my many temp jobs and on this job, in addition to my usual word processing, one of the things I had to do was to cut pictures out of magazines. This was a design firm and they had had a lot of their work published in design magazines and I was supposed to cut these pictures out with an Exacto knife. And this Exacto knife was making me feel really artistic. And I'd cut out the pictures and put them in portfolios, and I was loving this because with the Exacto knife and the portfolios I felt like I was really being creative, you know, like I was really exploiting my creative potential. And I had been doing this for a few days and I was getting really efficient and whipping down these pages and one day . . . I cut into my finger. And as soon as I did I went: *(Grasps finger with other hand)* and I thought, all right, I'm going to have to talk to someone about this. And I was working for very nice people in a one-room office and they were in a client meeting and I didn't want to interrupt them but I thought, Well, I'd better, so I went over to them and I said, "Excuse me, I'm sorry to bother you. This'll just take a sec. I'm sorry to interrupt. But I was wondering if you could tell me . . . have I cut the tip of my finger off?" And, of course, they were very concerned and they said, "Let's see." And I went like this: *(Holds out the cut finger with the other hand still wrapped around it.)* And they said, "Okay, you're going to have to take that other hand away." And I said, "Okay." *(Turns head away from finger and takes other hand away)* And they looked and they determined that I should go to the emergency room. And they asked if I was ready and I said, "Yes, I'm ready. I'm all ready. There's just one thing before we go. I'm just going to need to lie down here on the floor for a few minutes." And so I lay on the floor and I put my hand up in the air and they bandaged it up and then I was fine and I got in a cab and went to the hospital, I went to St. Vincent's. And when I got there I felt so stupid. Because here I was with my little cut finger and I looked around this room and there's somebody over here with a big bandage on their head, somebody over here with their arm in a sling, somebody over here with something in a . . . stained bag. And I felt so stupid with my little cut finger and I thought, I'm just going to go. But then I thought, No, I'm here, I'll just let the doctor look at it. So finally the doctor came and she unwrapped the finger. And she wanted to see how deep the cut was. And so she took a little stick . . .

Is everybody all right? Because if you need, we can just take a minute and all put our heads down between our legs. I just have to tell you, it's going to get a little worse before it gets better so if you need a minute, just say so. Okay? Okay, we'll just go on.

She wanted to see how deep the cut was so she took a little wooden stick and went . . . poke-ety, poke-ety, poke-ety, poke-ety, poke; poke-ety, poke-ety, poke-ety, poke-ety, poke; poke-ety, poke-ety, poke-ety, poke-ety, poke. And I said, "Excuse me. I'm just going to need to lay down here on the floor for just a minute." And she said, "Could you please wait just one second! . . . " Poke-ety, poke-ety, poke-ety, poke-ety, poke; poke-ety, poke-ety, poke-ety, poke-ety, poke; poke-ety, poke-ety, poke-ety, poke-ety, poke. And I said, "No, you know what? I'm going to have to lay down here on the floor right now." And she said, "Okay." And she got up and she went to the other side of the room because next to me there was a gurney, from which they had just removed some trauma patient and I think she was going to get a clean sheet for the gurney. But at that point I didn't really care what was on the gurney, I just knew I had to get on it. And I went over to it and I had one leg up, *(Stands on the bottom of stool, holding onto the back and lifts right leg up high, as if about to climb on the gurney)* about to get on the gurney when she saw me from across the room and screamed at me, "CAN YOU PLEASE WAIT JUST ONE MINUTE!" *(Hovers, frozen for a moment, with leg still in the air. Then acts out the following:)* And I went back to my chair. And I sat on my chair. And then I slid off my chair, onto the floor. And from out of my mouth I could hear this sound, *(Moaning and crawling downstage on her hands and knees)* "OH PLEASE! SOMEBODY HELP ME! CAN'T SOMEBODY HELP ME! CAN'T YOU SEE I'M SICK!? CAN'T YOU SEE I'M GOING TO DIE!? PLEASE! SOME-ONE HELP ME!"

(Crawls back to the chair and sits—exhausted, broken and hollow.)

I have come to accept that I have a part of me of which I am unconscious, that leads a parallel existence. A whole other set of behaviors that exhibit themselves to the world of which I am unaware. For instance, I am sitting on the couch doing an activity . . . *(Big yawn)* I'm sorry. Where was I? . . . I'm sit-ting and doing something . . . crocheting *(Another big yawn. Tries to shake it off)* I'm sorry. Oh, I hate it when I get sleepy in the theater! I was doing something . . . *(Starts to doze off)* Did I say this part already? *(Dozes off. Mutters a little in her sleep. She begins to slowly, almost imperceptibly, tilt to the right)* . . . and then that rabbit came over and . . .

(Laughs a laugh that gurgles out from deep in her dream. Her head has fallen back and she continues her slide to the right until her head hits the lamp shade and she wakes with a start.)

Oh.

(Wipes drool from the corner of her mouth and walks, disoriented, into a tight spotlight.)

I dreamed that Tracy was my friend. In the second grade I dreamed that Tracy was my best friend and the next day at school my heart leaped out of my chest when I saw her in the hall. "Hi! Tracy! Hi! Hi!" And Tracy, whom I had never particularly liked, looked at me like a hungry puppy being offered a milk bone. And she said, "Hi, Lisa. Hi. Hi." And I thought, Whoopsie.

(A brief dance of joy which ends at the graduation podium. The following speech is very showbizzy—for all the "little people out there.")

Hello everyone, class of 1979! The class of 1979 is Fine! Fine! Fine! My name is Lisa Kron. And I am so pleased to be here. I am just tickled to be here and I would like to thank . . . I'm sorry, honey. What's your name? Debby Downs! Let's give Debby Downs a big hand. Come on, give it up for Debbie Downs. Let me tell you something about this little lady. She is a real trooper. It wasn't easy for her to track down my manager and find a little window of time in my schedule when I was available to come here and perform for all of you, and let me tell you I am so pleased that I could work this in. I'm sorry . . . *(To Debby)* Didi, can you get me a Pellegrino? Thanks.

Let me fill you in on what I've been doing since I left here . . . Oh boy! Where to start, there's been so much . . . Well, going way back, college. I went to Kalamazoo College, right nearby. It was a tremendous experience. While I was there I studied theater in London for a while. It was an extraordinary program. I worked with people from the Royal Shakespeare Company and RADA and the National Theatre. I met Derek Jacobi. He's a terrific fellow. After that I toured with a national repertory company. It was a great, great experience. The artistic director of that company some of you might know. He's John Houseman who, of course, is a legend of the American theater but maybe some of you know him from that TV show in the '70s, *The Paper Chase*. And I know you people love TV so that's terrific. Since then I've moved to New York and it's been crazy. It's been shows and shows and touring and Europe a couple of times, it's been a whirlwind. But I want to take the focus off me for a second and put the focus on you. Especially those of you who decided not to leave Lansing, Michigan. You said, "See the world, adventures . . . it's not important to me. I'm going to stay right here in Lansing." I want to give you a big . . . I want you to give yourselves a big hand. I know that Dodie's been telling me about some of the creative projects you have going. I know the the ater community here is just doing a bang up job. On the way in, I passed the community college, and saw that you're doing *Cabaret*—again—and that's just terrific . . .

(Ends by punching the air and repeating "terrific!" Tapers off and becomes increasingly weary as she crosses to center.)

One day I was walking down the hall of my junior high school and I saw that there was a sanitary napkin laying in the hall by the vo-tech wing. It was a big one, the way they used to be big in 1979—kind of like a Depends diaper is now—which makes you wonder how big Depends diapers were in 1979. That pristine pad of cotton was lying in the hall in the morning when I got off the bus and at the end of the day it was in the exact same place. It lay in the main artery of the Dwight Rich Junior High School and was passed throughout the day by approximately two thousand people. And of course, the issue is not that no one noticed. And it's not what you might think, that people saw it through their peripheral vision but pretended not to. There was a lot of screaming and pointing going on. That's how I first noticed it. A crowd had gathered around what I assumed from the hysteria must be a severed limb. And the most interesting thing to me about all this is that no one picked it up all day. None of the kids picked it up which wasn't too surprising. These were junior high school students with a very low gross-out threshold. But none of the teachers picked it up. None of the administrators would touch it. And most revealing to me, none of the guidance counselors would be seen touching an unused sanitary pad in front of other people. The cooties on a sanitary pad are that strong—actually cross-generational.

Is everyone all right?

Okay, then let's go on to the fulcrum of this story, fraught with humiliation, i.e., the moment when some girl— we'll call her Cheryl—the moment when Cheryl reaches into her junior high purse for a Jolly Rancher, or some Juicy Fruit Gum, or maybe some change to buy a jumbo, double chocolate chip cookie for breakfast in the cafeteria—and as she pulls out her hand, out with it EXPLODES THE SANITARY PAD! Can you imagine? There must have been a frozen moment where everyone felt implicated. Until slowly, everyone else realizes that this happened to Cheryl, not to them. You can just see them starting to quietly comment and laugh and point just to make sure everyone knew that they were just standing there when— "POW! Cheryl's sanitary napkin flew right out of her underpants right on us!" That's not what happened, of course. But that's how Cheryl feels. And her face flattens into a white plate and she tries to make her body nonchalant which only makes it stiffen more, and she walks on down the hall, as if nothing happened. Nothing happened. And what's even worse is that all day, every time Cheryl walks down that hall she thinks, Surely it's gone by now. And all day, it's always there. And Cheryl begins to realize that that sanitary pad will be in the hall for the rest of her life, and that eventually they'll just build a big glass case around it with a brass plaque on it with her name on it— "Cheryl." And later in the day, when she passes that infamous spot in the hall, in spite of the fact that she knows everyone knows it was her that dropped it, Cheryl adopts the "who did that" attitude, well-known to anyone who ever passed gas in elementary school. And when she has to pass that spot in the hall, Cheryl points and laughs too and asks her friends if they have any idea who the idiot was who dropped a sanitary napkin in the hall.

(Crosses to the graduation podium. This following speech is delivered in a state of utter defeat and ineffectuality.)

Hello . . . Excuse me . . . hello . . . Debby, do you think that you could help me get their attention? Thanks. Hello. My name is Lisa Kron. And I am a member of the class of 1979. Some of you maybe, probably don't remember me. I wasn't very active in any of the activities here. Although, you know, I did work as the library page, during lunch time. And so, maybe if some of the rest of you also spent your lunch hour in the library you might recognize me from there. I'd like to thank Debby Downs for asking me here. Thank you, Debby. I really appreciate it. Although I don't know if my work is what you were expecting. I'm sure you've never seen me before. I've never been on TV or anything. I'll never be on TV. Because I'm a big lesbian. Although, maybe that's just an excuse. Maybe I'll never be on TV because I don't really have any talent and I just use being a lesbian as a big . . . crutch. I don't know. So, I'll tell you a little about what I do. I live in

New York City and I work as a performer and I do a lot of shows, but I still have a job as a word processor. And it's really exhausting. You know, I remember, before I left here I took a class with Richard Thomson at the BoarsHead Theater and I remember he said to us, you know, "If there's anything you can do with your life besides theater, do it because it's really hard." And, it's *really hard*. So, I'll just do a little of what I do. I tell stories. That's what I do. No big New York production like you might have been expecting, just story after story after story after story . . .

(Wanders back to the music stand.)

Number 17:
When I was in college there was a woman in the theater department named Gladys Butler who was like a theater booster. She was an older lady from the community. I think she was seven thousand years old and she looked like Margaret Hamilton if Margaret Hamilton had been rendered as a dried apple doll. Gladys was in a production of *You Can't Take it With You* that I was in also. I was playing Rheba the Black maid. Quite a stretch as you might imagine. Concerned as they were about racism at Kalamazoo College they changed the ethnicity of my character from Black to Irish. They didn't change any of the dialogue. So I still had to say lines like, "Yassuh, I sure is glad I'se colored." But I had to say them with a brogue. It went something like: *(She repeats the line with an Irish brogue).*

Gladys was a real crab apple. She'd say anything to anybody. My friend Dale and I thought she was a panic because it didn't phase her to ask the department head things like, did he have a pole up his ass or what. And we loved this because the head of our theater department was a very short man and his first name was Leslie and he took that out on us. And so we loved Gladys Butler and I have a complete soft spot for older ladies and I was completely captivated by Gladys. And one Sunday matinee day, she and I were in the wings, waiting for our cues and standing there in that twilight world of the dark looking out into the bright lights and I think I forgot for a moment that she was Gladys, the older lady from the community, and for one moment, seeing her in my peripheral vision I must have thought she was one of my lesbo college buddies because without thinking I leaned over and I kissed Gladys Butler on her neck. And then I remembered who she was and I thought, Oh my God! What have I done! There was a horrible second in which I waited for her to run onto the stage, point back at me and scream, "Stay away from me, you dirty lesbo!" I thought her forty matinee lady friends were going to leap out of their seats, point at me and scream, "Lesbian! Lesbian! You can't act and you're a lesbian." (You can see I was experiencing anxiety on a lot of levels at that time.) But Gladys didn't say anything. And, as a matter of fact, from that day forward Gladys Butler became completely devoted to me and she used to come and find me when I was in my classes and walk right in, interrupting the class, and bring me little gifts. And on the day that I graduated she gave me a little sculpture that she had made out of nuts with googily eyes glued on and a little sign on the bottom that said, "We're all nuts here."

(Curtain call music is "September" by Earth, Wind and Fire. During the second bow her hand hits the music stand and as she lurches to grab it, and the papers fly, the lights go to blackout.)

End of Play

Lisa Kron moved to New York City from Michigan in 1984, and after a lost year of Equity showcases and two seasons of summer stock, she found her way down to the OBIE Award-winning W.O.W. Café theater collective and began creating solo performances and working with the theater group that would eventually become The Five Lesbian Brothers.

Over the years, her work has been presented at New York Theatre Workshop, The Joseph Papp Public Theater/New York Shakespeare Festival, Serious Fun! at Lincoln Center (New York City), La Jolla Playhouse, American Repertory Theatre (Cambridge), A Contemporary Theatre (Seattle), Center Stage (Baltimore), U.C.L.A. Performance Series, Actors Theatre of Louisville, Yale Repertory Theatre (New Haven), Spoleto Festival U.S.A (Charleston), Trinity Repertory Company and Perishable Theatre (Providence), The Wexner Center for the Arts (Columbus), The W.O.W. Café, Dixon Place (New York City), Performance Space 122 (New York City), La MaMa Experimental Theatre Club (New York City) as well as the Barbican Centre in London and the Rinkogun Company in Tokyo.

With The Five Lesbian Brothers she has cowritten and appeared in four plays: *The Secretaries, Brave Smiles . . . another lesbian tragedy, Voyage to Lesbos* and *Brides of the Moon* which have been produced by New York Theatre Workshop, W.O.W. Café, Theatre Rhinoceros (San Francisco) and Diverse Works (Houston). An anthology of these plays, *Five Lesbian Brothers/Four Plays* was published by Theatre Communications Group (TCG) in June 2000.

2.5 Minute Ride received an OBIE Award, an L.A. Dramalogue Award, a GLAAD Media Award, the New York Press

Award for Best Autobiographical Show and Drama Desk and Outer Critics Circle nominations. *101 Humiliating Stories* received a Drama Desk nomination. Other awards include a 2000 NEA/TCG Theatre Residency Program for Playwrights grant, development grants from the Creative Capital Foundation, the 1997 Cal Arts/Alpert Award in Theater, a New York Foundation for the Arts Fellowship in playwriting and the Robert Chesley Gay and Lesbian Playwriting Award.

As an actress Lisa has appeared in many productions, including Paul Rudnick's *The Most Fabulous Story Ever Told* at New York Theatre Workshop and the Minetta Lane theater, *The Vagina Monologues* and workshop productions of Paula Vogel's *The Mineola Twins* at New York Theatre Workshop and American Repertory Theatre.